Praise for
The Alphabet of Grief

"Reading Andrea Raynor's *Alphabet of Grief* is like sitting down for a cup of coffee with a wise and gentle friend. Raynor understands what it means to grieve, and she reminds us of the larger wisdom of our faith and the story of our lives. After a loved one dies, my patients' families sometimes wish there was a chaplain in the community they could call for guidance and comfort after the hospice team says goodbye. Now I can give them this book. It is wise, luminous, down to earth, and enormously comforting."

— KERRY EGAN, author of *On Living* and *Fumbling*

"There are no perfect words when someone grieves, which is why *The Alphabet of Grief* provides a wonderful way to move through the process with bite-sized wisdoms. Raynor's personal, alphabetical blueprint allows us to take sorrow and loss at our own pace to come out on the other side."

— LEE WOODRUFF, *New York Times* best-selling author

"Andrea gently guides the reader through the ins and outs of grief. This book teaches what you may experience in grief and how to help someone navigate through it. Knowing profound grief myself, I found comfort in the words *living on* as a way to honor my son Chase."

— REBECCA KOWALSKI, mother of seven-year-old Chase who lost his life in the Sandy Hook Elementary tragedy

"In this compelling and comforting book, Andrea Raynor uses her finely honed wisdom from years of ministering to the grieving to accompany us down a path of exploration and healing. You will nod in recognition of the truth being shared and shed healing tears of gratitude for the profundity in these pages."

—FATHER EDWARD L. BECK, CP, CNN religion commentator and author of *God Underneath: Spiritual Memoirs of a Catholic Priest*

"Each short essay in *The Alphabet of Grief* is profoundly moving and insightful. For example, Andrea's piece on 'Dinner' becomes nearly luminous as she narrates how death redefines our ordinary. We linger with her in such vivid detail that the helpful meditations and affirmations at the end of each section arrive almost as an afterthought. As a health-care chaplain, Andrea has a wealth of experiences to draw upon, but she doesn't hold back personally, bravely processing her own grief for her father. You and I are the recipients of this treasure."

—RT. REV. GEORGE E. PACKARD, retired bishop for the armed services and federal ministries, the Episcopal Church

"Compassionate and inspiring, *The Alphabet of Grief* provides a framework to process the multifaceted emotions surrounding the loss of a loved one. Raynor empathically caresses our bleeding hearts and gives practical suggestions to soothe our pain. This book is a blessing to anyone who has ever lost a loved one. For those who have been spared such a loss, Raynor's words will reaffirm the commitment to love with abandon."

—THERESA JOSEPH, coauthor of *Everyday Mystic: Finding the Extraordinary in the Ordinary*

"A beautifully written self-care guide to live by when a loved one has died, this book offers practical wisdom I will use on a daily basis when counseling hospice families in anticipation of the death of a beloved. Andrea's inspirational stories will help the grieving make sense of their personal expression of emotions during this sacred and vulnerable time."

—MARY LANDBERG, hospice RN, MPH, and CHPN and
  author of *Enduring Love: Inspiring Stories of Love and
  Wisdom at the End of Life*

"Andrea Raynor's thoughts and words lead the reader to understand death and love in a new way—the way that leads to healing. I commend this book to those who are grieving, to those who help others going through that journey, and to professionals who may use it as a resource."

—REV. DR. BILL SHILLADY, executive director of the United
  Methodist City Society

"Andrea Raynor writes about grief with such compassion that you'll feel as if she has wrapped you in a warm blanket. Her alphabet touches on all aspects of grief. In acknowledging the breadth and depth, Raynor shows us that we will get through it, each at our own pace. Everyone who has suffered a loss should read this book."

—ANNABEL MONAGHAN, author of *Does This Volvo Make
  My Butt Look Big?*

THE
ALPHABET
OF
GRIEF

THE

ALPHABET

OF

GRIEF

Words to Help in Times of Sorrow

ANDREA RAYNOR

WATERBROOK

THE ALPHABET OF GRIEF

All Scripture quotations are taken from the Holy Bible, New International Version®, NIV®. Copyright © 1973, 1978, 1984, 2011 by Biblica Inc.® Used by permission. All rights reserved worldwide.

Details in some anecdotes and stories have been changed to protect the identities of the persons involved.

Hardcover ISBN 978-0-7352-9029-7
eBook ISBN 978-0-7352-9030-3

Copyright © 2017 by Andrea Raynor

Cover design by Mark D. Ford

Published in the United States by WaterBrook, an imprint of the Crown Publishing Group, a division of Penguin Random House LLC, New York.

WATERBROOK® and its deer colophon are registered trademarks of Penguin Random House LLC.

Library of Congress Cataloging-in-Publication Data
Names: Raynor, Andrea, author.
Title: The alphabet of grief : words to help in times of sorrow / Andrea Raynor.
Description: First Edition. | Colorado Springs, Colorado : WaterBrook, 2017. |
Identifiers: LCCN 2017008983 (print) | LCCN 2017030046 (ebook) | ISBN 9780735290303 (electronic) | ISBN 9780735290297 (hardcover)
Subjects: LCSH: Grief—Religious aspects—Christianity. | Bereavement—Religious aspects—Christianity.
Classification: LCC BV4909 (ebook) | LCC BV4909 .R39 2017 (print) | DDC 242/.4—dc23
LC record available at https://lccn.loc.gov/2017008983

Printed in the United States of America
2017—First Edition

10 9 8 7 6 5 4 3 2 1

SPECIAL SALES

Most WaterBrook books are available at special quantity discounts when purchased in bulk by corporations, organizations, and special-interest groups. Custom imprinting or excerpting can also be done to fit special needs. For information, please e-mail specialmarketscms@penguinrandomhouse.com or call 1-800-603-7051.

For Sorcha
Grief brought you to me—
love keeps you close.

The life given us by nature is short, but the memory of a well-spent life is eternal.

—Marcus Tullius Cicero

Contents

Preface   xv

Absence   1
Bereavement   4
Crying   7
Dinner   11
Everyone Else   16
Forever   21
Ghosts   25
Home   32
Isolation   37
Joy   42
Kinship   47
Loneliness   52
Moving On   58

Night   62
Out of Body   68
Partings   72
Quilt   80
Rainbows   84
Sayings   90
Treasure   98
Until   103
Violence   109
Why   117
Xs and Os   124
Yesterday   129
Zzzz   136

Acknowledgments   143

Preface

We all yearn for comfort when someone we love dies. In the imme-diate aftermath of death, we may find it in the company of friends and family or in the rituals of faith. But when the funeral services are over, when friends leave and the house grows quiet, many are left floundering. The unchangeable reality of loss looms like a shadow in our every days. We can feel lost and alone, even when surrounded by people who love us. Things we thought might offer some small mea-sure of solace, or at least distraction, often fall miserably short. To what do we turn? It's rarely television—and music is often too potent an emotional trigger—so many reach for a book. When one is griev-ing, however, reading is quite a different experience than it was before. Those who once considered themselves voracious readers discover they cannot take in more than a few pages before losing focus. Most don't want a treatise on grief. They don't want to be educated, particularly, and they certainly don't want platitudes. They want a few simple thoughts or images to hold on to, a few stepping-stones across the river of sadness.

The Alphabet of Grief was written for this purpose: to offer sim-ple but thoughtful reflections to ease the isolation and loneliness of grief. Using the letters of the alphabet as rungs on the ladder of sorrow, I chose each word based on the countless hours I have spent with grieving people. Not only have they shared with me the pain of loss but they have also taught me about the daunting and sometimes mysterious journey of living. It is for them—for every face around the bereavement table, for everyone who has known loss—and for you that I have written this book.

> Absence is to love what wind is to fire; it
> extinguishes the small, it enkindles the great.
>
> —Roger de Bussy-Rabutin

Absence

Just as silence can be deafening, absence can be full of presence. This is often the case after someone dies, although it may take some time to notice. The absence of one we love can press in on us, swallowing us like Jonah in the belly of the whale. When will we be spit out? When will this suffering, this darkness, cease? We listen for the phone to ring. We wait for the doorknob to turn and a familiar voice to call "I'm home!" And each moment we must take a deep breath and remind ourselves of the one thing we cannot have: the physical presence of our loved ones.

Since my father's death, my mother cannot bring herself to sit on the stool in the kitchen where he sat as they sipped their morning coffee. Nor can she curl up in the chair in the family room where he fell asleep virtually every night watching TV. In some ways, this accentuates his absence—the empty chair, the empty place at the table—but in other ways, the space is filled with his presence. I sit on his stool and gaze out the kitchen window, imagining his eyes taking in the blue of the sky or a bird in flight. I look at my mother reading the paper and can feel how she held my father's gaze, sitting there, elbow to elbow for almost sixty years. The hole left by his death is so profound that we begin to fill it with our longing, with our tears, and with our memories.

And yet, somehow, the heightened awareness of his absence mysteriously invokes the comfort of his presence. Like the reflection of a mountain on a still and pristine lake, he is here and not here. We are learning to live with the reflection of him. I see him reflected in my mother's tender words and in the life they shared together. My mother sees him in the way I think, in my son's athleticism, my daughter's creativity, my sister's flashing brown eyes, and in the specks of him scattered like stardust in our family and in the writings he left behind.

A reflection is no substitute for the real thing, but it can sometimes summon an aspect of the ones we are missing. It can trigger a sensory memory; it can make the distance between them and us feel not so terribly far. Instead of saying, for example, "He is not here. She is not here," we can look for the parts of them that remain. They live in our stories and in the ways our souls are connected in love. Because we can no longer hold their hands, sometimes it helps to hold something that belonged to them in order to cope with their absence. We wrap ourselves in her sweater, we wear his watch, we cuddle her beloved stuffed bear. One woman I know takes her husband's cane with her when she goes on errands. "I know it's silly," she tells me, "but having it there next to me in the car makes me feel less alone. If I'm going out, I say, 'Come on, Vin, we're going to the store.'" Her husband's cane is a touchstone for her. By itself, it is just a cane. Imbued with her memories, it is a talisman that has the power to draw her husband near again.

We cannot change the fact that our loved ones are physically absent from us, no matter how much we hurt, no matter how much we protest or shake our fists at the heavens, but we can look for them in the clues they have left behind. The broken heart is never empty; it has been cracked open. And flowing from the cracks is a love that rises like an eternal spring within us. Nothing will replace the warmth of my father's hand resting on my mother's—but his presence fills the silence as she remembers.

Meditation: Today I will try to feel the presence of my loved one as strongly as I feel the absence. I will visualize a happy, perhaps even insignificant moment, remembering every detail, until warmth begins to fill my heart center.

Affirmation: Although my loved one is absent, I will open my heart to happy memories.

The world breaks everyone and afterward
many are strong at the broken places.

—Ernest Hemingway, *A Farewell to Arms*

Bereavement

Bereavement is often thought of as a set period in one's life after the death of a loved one, rather than the state of being sad. A *time of bereavement* implies that it is finite, that grief is something to be gotten over, that the least affected can go back to their lives and, by implication, so should you who are grieving.

Many people are uncomfortable with what cannot be fixed. They are squeamish about other people's tears and are often at a loss for what to say to someone who is grieving. Some begin to avoid the friend or coworker who has suffered a loss and (intentionally or not) convey a thinly veiled impatience for life to return to normal—something that no longer exists for those whose lives have been rocked by death. People are uncomfortable with grief because they are uncomfortable with death. Death is embarrassing, a failure of sorts, and certainly an inconvenience to others. Some recoil, as if misfortune might be contagious, and others keep their distance, telling themselves it is "out of respect."

During the first month after a death, the bereaved are usually treated with understanding. Most workplaces grant a few days of paid bereavement leave, and airlines offer a small break for close family members to travel to funerals. After about thirty days, however, we are expected to get on with it—with life, with our routines, with happiness, and with how we have always been. The only problem is, everything has changed. What's more, we have not chosen this change. It has chosen us. We have been catapulted, without a map, into a frightening territory called "the new normal."

When people show up for a bereavement group for the first time, many are in post-traumatic shock. Death is shocking. Grief is shocking. Usually someone in the group has had Elisabeth Kübler-Ross's *On Death and Dying* thrust into her hands with the implied reassurance that the five stages of grief can be moved through systematically, like a set of operating instructions or an emotional checklist. But bereavement isn't linear. It doesn't move in a smooth upward arc. It is jagged and irregular. It probably wasn't Kübler-Ross's intention to create rigid stages, but we tend to interpret her work that way. We like clear-cut, systematic plans. We like how-to guides and "five easy steps" and "ten ways to . . ." Those who suddenly find themselves back in the anger stage, for instance, sometimes think they are failing in the grieving process. They wonder, *Shouldn't I be further along? Am I going backwards? Didn't I do this already?* When the pressure is taken off, when people are told that they can grieve for as long as they want, in whatever way they want, there is a collective exhale. We don't get graded on our grief.

I'm not sure why bereavement groups help; I just know that they can. Perhaps life is less lonely in the company of others who have loved deeply, who mourn deeply, and who have the courage to show up, to tell their stories, and to hear the stories of others. It is both staggering and humbling to witness such tender exchanges among the broken-hearted. Attending a bereavement group is not for everyone, and not every bereavement group is helpful. Grief is both personal and universal. Your loss is as unique as the person you are grieving—and yet everyone who dares to love will know loss. For many people, bereavement will not come to an end, but the sharp edges will grow smooth with time. When this happens, grief itself will become a familiar friend, one who will walk beside you as a guardian of love.

Meditation: Today I will treat myself gently as I grieve. I will not pressure myself to feel better but will accept that I am doing the best I can.

Affirmation: I will honor my bereavement as a sacred journey.

Deep in earth my love is lying
And I must weep alone.

—Edgar Allan Poe

Crying

When I told my sister Jennie that I had accepted a job as a hospice chaplain, the first thing she said was, "That's a *terrible* job for you! You cry at the drop of a hat." She was right, of course—not about it being a terrible job for me but about my tendency to cry easily. My dad was the same way. We'd both cry at the ending of a movie we'd seen countless times or while telling a story that had moved us. Before Dad died, I'd seen my mom cry precisely three times: once at the death of a friend's child, once at her brother's funeral, and once when she was pregnant with my little brother and someone accidentally shrunk a handmade baby blanket. I can pretty much chalk that last one up to hormones. Now, however, her tears flow freely and frequently.

After working with the dying for almost twenty years, I have cried a lot, albeit mostly out of sight. It's not that I'm ashamed of my tears, but what I have found is that they can be a distraction. It's hard to be fully present for another when in the throes of one's own emotion. And so, in the midst of heartbreak, I take a deep breath and focus on what might be most helpful to the family whose loved one is dying or has died. The last thing I want is to intrude on a moment that is not primarily mine.

I have also witnessed this mysterious ebb and flow of emotions, of crying and comfort, among people who are grieving. If one person begins to cry during a bereavement session, for example, others seem to shift fairly quickly into concern and support. There is a sort of turn taking when it comes to expressing deep grief, as if we all know intuitively that someone has to remain on dry land to prevent everyone else from getting washed away. Though my heart breaks to see my mother cry, for example, I can usually remain steady in the face of her pain. If *I* cry, on the other hand, she instinctually digs into the deep reservoir of who she is as a mother so that we do not go tumbling over the falls together.

No one likes to cry in public. It's embarrassing. When the walls that hold our shaky insides suddenly come crashing down, we feel vulnerable and exposed. A song comes on the radio stopping us in our tracks; we reach for peanut butter at the grocery store before remembering that it was our loved one who liked peanut butter; we turn to say something about the headline in the newspaper and realize no one's there. Tears can come like a tidal wave when we least expect it. But even a tsunami of tears does subside eventually, whether we want it to or not. Sometimes this is scary. Crying keeps the blade of grief sharp and, therefore, the event of our loved ones' deaths close. When we stop crying, does it mean that we have let them go? Some fear this, and so they hold on to their tears and to the fresh wound that death has imparted.

Crying can be cathartic or it can just be—but tears do not tether our loved ones to us. They do not create a river we can swim across to reach them. Instead, they sometimes block our view of the very people we agonize to see. As C. S. Lewis wrote after the death of his wife,

> And suddenly at the very moment when, so far, I mourned H. least, I remembered her best. Indeed it was something (almost) better than memory; an instantaneous, unanswerable impression. To say it was like a meeting would be going too far. Yet there was that in it which tempts one to use those words. It was as if the lifting of the sorrow removed a barrier. . . . You can't see anything properly while your eyes are blurred with tears.*

In the midst of death, it's understandable to cry an ocean of tears. But our loved ones will never be found in our sorrow, for they exist now in joy. They are at home with God, where there is no sorrow, no suffering, no pain. That is the promise that is ours in faith. In joy is where we will find them, and that is where we will see them most clearly.

---

* C. S. Lewis, *A Grief Observed,* paperback ed. (New York: HarperCollins, 1994), 62–63.

Meditation: Today I will cry if I feel like crying. But when the tears subside, I will take a deep breath and open myself to the possibility of experiencing the happy presence of my loved one.

Affirmation: Like a rainbow after a storm, joy can follow sorrow when I trust that my loved one is with God.

There is only one difference between a long life and a good dinner: that, in the dinner, the sweets come last.

—Robert Louis Stevenson

Dinner

Dinnertime can be the hardest time of the day after the death of a loved one. The empty place at the table looms like a neon sign, silently broadcasting its vacancy, night after night without ceasing. It is a place that will never be filled. Lifelong couples, especially those who have shared children, come to accept the gradual shrinking of the table as these children grow up and leave the nest, but the table still has an accordion quality. Leaves can be added when the family gathers and taken away when adult children and grandchildren go home. When the last family member leaves and the house grows quiet, what remains is the comfort of two place settings, evidence of a hand to hold at the end of the day, proof that we are not left to face the world alone—that is, until we are.

What was once taken for granted, the simple act of eating, can become a dreaded activity. It's as if we've suddenly been thrust into a foreign land whose customs are strange and daunting. For many, going out to dinner is no longer an option. The thought of sitting at a table for one is excruciating, and trying to make dinner conversation with friends often requires too much effort. Feeling like the third wheel can also inhibit those who are grieving from socializing. When a child dies, the empty place creates an irreparable hole in the fabric of the family. The table is broken and the bridge to the future has been blown to bits. It is not history that is lost so much as possibility for parents who lose a child. The ghost tingles from this part of the soul's amputation will be felt for generations.

So, what to do? Obviously there are no easy answers for how to handle dinnertime. The body needs to eat, even if the spirit is lethargic and uninterested in food. Some find that having a radio on helps to fill the void. Others watch something on the television while they eat. Still others hardly eat at all. People who used to enjoy cooking find themselves nibbling cheese and crackers, and others make due with microwavable meals. The dinner table symbolizes daily sustenance and reconnection after the trials of the day, and it can highlight the loss of our loved ones as almost nothing else can.

If I shut my eyes, I can picture the family dinner table of my childhood. We fit eight around the table in our small kitchen, with always room for more. The conversation was raucous and lively. My father queried each of us children about our day, about what we were learning and what was on our minds, his laser gaze both intense and dancing. I can return to my place there at the table in the whisper of a heartbeat. The images make me smile as I listen for the snippets of conversation that still float in my memory. I can hear the clatter of silverware and the shifting of ice in the glasses, can feel the damp steam rising from the stove, and can taste the mashed potatoes with my mother's dark, delicious gravy.

But now my mother sits alone, small and silent in her kitchen. If only she could see that we are all there in spirit, our voices bouncing off the walls and fanning out to infinity in endless circles. If she listened, perhaps she could hear the echoes of our family life and could feel the love that continues to reverberate. Happiness would conjure my father to preside with his laughing eyes and his reassurance that she is never, in fact, alone. He would take her hand and say, "Let's pray."

We always said grace at the table before lifting our forks. It was a way to acknowledge our blessings, to give thanks for the food and for every gift of love and life that we shared. Bowing our heads was a way to recognize, somehow, that we were not in charge, that the blessing of each day and of the simple gift of food should be counted. Sometimes we held hands, sometimes we sang, sometimes we took turns offering the prayer. Starting the meal with an expression of gratitude set the tone. It eliminated any grumblings about leftovers or not liking the tuna casserole. It grounded us in love.

When we are grieving, we sometimes forget to give thanks. So much, it seems, has been taken away. Of course we miss the companionship and the company of those we love, but we can invite God to join us at the table, to fill the empty space, and to provide us with needed sustenance. We must feed our spirits if we are to survive in bodies that are famished by grief. At some point, we have to make the choice to live. One way to do this is to hear in the silence the scraping of plates, the echo of satisfied sighs and of every meal shared. Embedded in the essence of who we are is the company of our loved ones, a veritable feast for which we can give thanks. One thing we can be sure of is the security of what has been. I am no less my children's mother now, for instance, as when I fed them at my breast, their private table for one. No distance, not even my death, could ever diminish this. And when I am no longer here, I pray they will fill their plates with the love that I have left them and that which continues to flow.

Perhaps if we took a moment to bow our heads, we would dread less the empty place when we open our eyes. Beginning from a place of abundance, recognizing all the blessings we have known, we might dine like kings and queens. When we feel grateful, we feel connected, whole, accompanied. "Gratitude bestows reverence," Milton wrote long ago, "allowing us to encounter everyday epiphanies, those transcendent moments of awe that change forever how we experience life and the world."

When we remember to give thanks, we open ourselves up to a different way of seeing, a different way of moving through our sorrow. Recognizing our blessings, especially the love we have known, and dining with the One from whom all blessings flow help us transcend our grief. And transcendence leads to awe, and awe drops us to our knees. Gratitude fills both the empty plate and the empty place. When someone we love is missing from the table, it alone can sweeten the end of a dinner.

Meditation: Today I will invite God to dine with me. I will recognize the fullness rather than the emptiness at my table, and give thanks.

Affirmation: I will nurture my body as well as my spirit. I am never alone at the table.

Can I see another's woe,
And not be in sorrow too?
Can I see another's grief,
And not seek for kind relief?

—William Blake

Everyone Else

He was nine years old the day they buried his mother. It was also his sister's thirteenth birthday, but no one seemed to notice. These were stoic times, times when death threatened to darken every door and the grief of children was seldom taken into account or even acknowledged. It was 1944 and there was a war going on. Sons and husbands were dying on distant shores, and entire families were being rounded up and murdered. Still, this was *his* mother. She died quietly at home after an illness that no one seemed to fully understand. There would be no folded American flag, no taps played, no twenty-one-gun salute. She slipped away, taking part of him with her—but life went on for everyone else. How could this be?

My father's voice would still shake and his eyes fill with tears as he recounted this day, now many long years in the past. Among the images made vividly clear when he spoke was that of riding to the cemetery on the way to bury his mother. It was a hot August day, a day when other children were out playing and mothers were busy mothering and the Allies were winning and the mood was hopeful and life was normal. If only he could jump out of the car and be one of them, he thought. He wanted to be one of the boys who were playing and would hear their mothers' voices calling them home for dinner at the end of the day, but he couldn't. He was riding in a black car, just behind the one that carried his mother's silent body. Beyond the window was a world he did not know, one populated by a people called *everyone else*.

When someone we love dies, our world comes screeching to a stop—even though life continues on around us. It can feel cruel and surreal to know that others are going about their days as usual when ours will never be the same. I will always remember sitting in the hospital with the body of an eighteen-year-old boy, a boy I had known since he was five years old. It was supposed to be just another Saturday night, one spent hanging out with lifelong friends. Sure, they partied a little, but he was home in bed by eleven o'clock. The next morning, he didn't wake up. He was brought to the hospital just barely alive. I held vigil with the family as they sat by his side, while numerous friends waited in the next room, still clinging to hope till the end. The day was gray and gloomy, mirroring the somber mood of those gathered. We watched him float further and further out to sea, like a sailboat on the ocean, until the lapping waves of his breath came no more. At that moment, the room suddenly became drenched in sunlight. It was as if, in leaving the body, his spirit temporarily illuminated the room before moving on. After-wards, he lay frozen in his perfection, his youthful, athletic frame exuding a lingering vitality that was at once defiant and defeated in the face of death.

I offered to sit with him until the medical personnel came to take his body. It was the least I could do. His devastated parents could bear no more, and they certainly did not need the image burned in their minds of their son being taken away. The father of the boy led his wife out of the room, her body leaning heavily against his. "He's gone," his mother had said when I asked if she was ready to leave the hospital. "He's gone." This was true—but so was the fact that it felt wrong to leave him alone there. For the next couple of hours, I held his hand, stroked his forehead, and spoke to him. And I prayed. He was just a year ahead of my son, and at that moment, I felt like a stand-in for every parent who has lost a child.

In the middle of this quiet communion, I heard loud voices com-ing from the nurses' station. They weren't loud as in the case of a medical emergency; they were happy loud, laughing loud. They were the sound of *everyone else,* and their banter went through me like a dagger. I felt like a mother who was trying to get her baby to sleep. I felt like a mother whose baby was not going to wake up. *Don't they know that a boy has just died in here?* It hit a nerve, a primitive nerve of protection and outrage. The longer it went on, the angrier I be-came. My only comfort was in the fact that the boy's mother had al-ready gone. I would have been horrified if she'd had to experience this.

I walked out into the hall and approached the nurses' station, hackles up. They were probably in the middle of a shift change, but I didn't care. "Excuse me," I said, barely containing my fury, "do you not know that an eighteen-year-old boy just died, that his body is still lying in that room, and that your loud voices and laughter feel terribly callous and rude?" They immediately apologized and changed their demeanor, but it didn't feel entirely genuine. They still lived in that world where bad things happen to other people. Before walking away, I stopped and turned to them. "You know, I could have been his mother sitting there."

In some ways, at that moment, I was his mother. I was doing for her what she could not do, thereby shifting some of the burden of grief off of her broken shoulders. My offer to sit with her son took away only a thimbleful of her ocean of grief, but it spared her images I'm glad she doesn't have and gave her another mother's hand to hold. Her grief is singular, as all of our losses are singular. No one will ever be able to touch the depth of that pain, or of any parent who has lost a child, or child who has lost a parent. Because we can't touch it, however, does not mean we should turn our backs. It doesn't mean we should leave the bereaved alone in their pain. Just because we cannot fix something does not mean we cannot help. The more we lovingly and tenderly reach for each other, the less isolating grief will feel. There is no "us" and "them" when it comes to death—not in the long run. Walking together, we can make it our intention to be part of *everybody*—every mother, every father, every child who is in pain—rather than being *everybody else*. And when it comes our time to grieve, chances are we, too, will have a hand to hold.

Meditation: Today I will try not to isolate myself in my grief. I will ask for help when I need it and will open myself to others who wish to ease my burden or who also need a hand to hold.

Affirmation: When my heart is broken, I will let others in. When I see others in pain, I will offer my broken heart.

You gave me a forever within the numbered days.

—John Green, *The Fault in Our Stars*

Forever

Birth and death are like the number twelve on a clock. It's where the second hand starts and finishes, moving both away from and toward the same place. What happens in between, as it descends and ascends, makes up a minute, an hour, a life. We don't know where the spirit comes from or where it goes when we die, but people of faith sense some kind of circular flow, a portal from and to the Divine. Life passes in an instant—and suddenly we are confronted with the difference between eternity and forever. Eternity is what we hope to experience with our loved ones when our second hand reaches twelve again. Forever is the time it takes to get there, the time left living without them here on earth.

Time is elusive. Days can seem endless and yet the years pass quickly. I found this when my children were babies. What might feel like three in the afternoon was often, in reality, only eleven in the morning—and yet, in the blink of an eye, they are now in their twenties. Similarly, when in the throes of grief, the hours can drag as we wait for the sound of feet that will never come. But the next thing we know, months or years have gone by. "I never thought I could live this long without your father," my mother says with a sigh. I sense the disappointment in her voice. They had always hoped to die together, or at least close together, but that has not been the case. For her and for many, the vow "to love and to cherish until death do us part" was a bit shortsighted. Death is not the finish line; love does not cease with death.

What do we do with the forever that separates us from our loved ones? It is a daunting proposition. Even if we have complete faith that we will one day be reunited, we must find a way to cope with their absence for the duration of our earthly lives. Part of us is like the child who, when told his pet had died, nodded in understanding before asking, "But when is she coming alive again?" Or the one who said to her grandmother, "Grandma, I know that Grandpa is in heaven, but I'm tired of him being there. Don't you think it's about time he came home?" When death comes, we have no choice but to accept it. It is an event that has happened at a specific moment in time, marked by a date and confirmed by all the rituals and legalities that follow. Forever, on the other hand, is something the heart cannot immediately comprehend. The full weight of forever can feel like a ship slowly taking on water: each day it becomes more apparent, and a feeling of helplessness in the face of it sometimes threatens to sink us.

Compounding the pain of forever are all the nevers that accompany it: I will never see him again; she will never walk through the door. I will never hear "Hey, Mom." These thoughts can run on a painful endless loop as we go about our days, like a record that keeps skipping back to the same terrible place. It's difficult to move forward when we dwell on that which cannot be changed. If we remain too long in the shadow of what has happened, we can become shadows ourselves. Sometimes we are searching for our loved ones, sometimes for a part of ourselves, for the people we were before this loss. But our loved ones cannot be found in the darkness of never because they exist now in the light of eternity.

The flip side of never is always. Always transcends never, and it opens the future like a sunbeam breaking through a stormy sky. A small band of friends, mourning an unfathomable loss, experienced this over two thousand years ago. In the mountains of Galilee they gathered, hardly daring to hope for the impossible: that death did not have the final word. They were scared, they were exhausted, they doubted. In the darkness of their despair, Jesus appeared, offering this reassurance to his grief-stricken disciples: "And surely I am with you *always,* to the very end of the age."* The always that Jesus promises is stronger than death and points the way to eternity.

Instead of staying entrenched in the painful forever that separates us from our loved ones, we can choose to dwell in the promise of always. We will always be accompanied. We will always have the love we've known, the experiences, the joy, and the intimate, special moments we've cherished with those who have died. We can always listen in our hearts for the voices that are dear and familiar, for those that continue to speak to us in our dreams, and for that of the Wonderful

---

* Matthew 28:20, emphasis added.

Counselor, who is ever present to console us. We can face our forevers because we know that our loved ones are with us, that God is with us, and what awaits beyond our earthly forever is an eternity of together.

Meditation: Today I will fill my forever with joyful memories and will move with courage through my numbered days.

Affirmation: With faith, I trust that I will one day be reunited with my loved one in eternity.

I know that ghosts *have* wandered on earth. Be with
me always—take any form—drive me mad! only *do*
not leave me in this abyss, where I cannot find you!

—Emily Brontë, *Wuthering Heights*

Ghosts

Death can make even the most skeptical person a believer in ghosts.
One might say that this is because we are desperate to experience the
presence of our loved ones again, that our desire for communication
with them outweighs rationality, and that grief plays tricks on the
mind. But those who sit around a bereavement table, and those who
have lost dear ones, can find this explanation lacking. Whether they
adhere to a particular faith, especially one that upholds the idea of an
afterlife, or are not religious at all, people who grieve are often open to
mystery. Perhaps death is so jarring that it unhinges our perceptions.
It strikes with a deep and terrifying rumble—like an earthquake—
tumbling the familiar walls of our existence and shaking our founda-
tions. When the dust clears, what is left of our lives can seem utterly
unrecognizable, at least for a time. The world we can see and feel and
hear and touch, the one we can identify by smell, becomes less important in the immediate aftermath of grief than both the one that has

been destroyed and the one just beyond our grasp—the one where our loved ones have gone.

The question is, *where* have they gone? Those with little in common besides their grief find comfort in the possibility that life continues in some form and that the veil between this world and the next is not only thin, it is permeable. Whether this is wishful thinking or spiritual reality, who can say for sure? Those who share unexplainable phenomenon relating to their departed loved ones give hope to those who yearn for such experiences. Even those who doubt the authenticity of these accounts can find themselves spiritually curious, perhaps for the first time. Death seems to open a portal for some and creates questions for others. Most of us hunger for certainties and for reassurance—but these are elusive when it comes to death. Like Thomas, forever known as the doubting disciple, we cannot seem to believe unless it happens to us, until the chill goes down our spines, until we smell our mother's perfume in an empty room or the light bulb flickers just when we say her name. We want to believe the chance of continued connection exists, but we are also afraid that the only answer to our shouts in the dark will be the echo of our own voices. Having faith in what we cannot see is easier said than done.

Maybe this is why we love ghost stories: they keep the door ajar to possibility. Ghost stories told around a campfire, however, are different from those told around a bereavement table. The former are usually scary, giving ghosts a rather bad rap; the latter aim to bring our loved ones near. Most of us do not want to be visited by ghosts, but we yearn for a visit or a sign from those we have lost. Love has a way of turning ghosts into angels. If I had recorded every experience that people have shared with me over the past twenty years about visitations from their angels, the book would be thick and difficult to disregard. It might even make a believer of the most skeptical. In some ways, I'm glad I did not. Belief is the precursor to faith, and faith isn't something one can be talked into. Faith has to ensue, igniting from within. Still, even the heart of a skeptic sometimes quickens when listening to someone speak about a mystical experience. *Maybe,* they think, *just maybe it's true!*

The stories shared by those who are grieving usually start sheepishly with something like, "You all might think I'm crazy but . . ." and, before long, heads are nodding and knowing looks are exchanged. Sometimes the stories are about a loved one who appears in a dream. These stories are readily accepted, envied even. One does not have to believe in an afterlife or communication with the dead to appreciate the comfort that dreams can bring. After my mother's best friend lost her six-year-old son, I remember her saying how much she treasured the dreams in which he would appear. "During those times, I feel as though I am with him again," she would say. "I can feel him in my arms and can hear his voice. When I feel myself starting to wake up, I struggle to stay in the dream because that's where Matthew comes to me. That's where we're together."

Other stories involve goose bumps, the kind caused by the sudden awareness that a loved one might be near. These, of course, cannot be proven, but they bring immense comfort to both listener and teller. "I was just sitting on the couch when I had the profound sense that my husband was right beside me," says one woman. "Yes," says another, "that happens to me sometimes when I least expect it. I suddenly feel this warmth around me and I know that he's there." Are these women crazy? Imagining things? I would like to think that we never know enough to say something is impossible, especially when it comes to the spiritual realm. I have had numerous experiences myself that point toward mystery. These still have a way of startling me, even as they confirm my strong conviction that we are not alone. This is especially true when we are grieving. As a Christian, I believe the Holy Spirit accompanies me through my days. Isn't it possible, then, that the Spirit brings a friend from time to time, namely someone I am missing?

While making one of my routine drives from New York to Ohio to see my son Alex play football, I had one of these mystical experiences. For me, the road is a perfect place to reflect, to pray, and to open myself to inspiration. I spend much of the nine hours in silence, rarely turning on the radio and talking on the phone as little as possible. It's a time to clear my head and to take in the natural beauty of the hills, the sunset, and the changing sky. On this particular trip, I was thinking about how proud my dad would have been to see his grandson play college football. I thought of Alex's tattoo, the one with my father's signature, how he touched it before each game and how he felt his Poppie watching over him. Before I could stop it, the well burst and I found myself sobbing in the car. It was like a thunderstorm that strikes without warning. I had no choice but to let the tears fall. I didn't try to hold them back or talk myself out of it; I just let them flow. Maybe I allowed myself the luxury of crying because I was alone. It also helped that my car was literally and figuratively propelling me forward, preventing any chance of getting stuck in the past or in the eddy of emotion. I was safe to let my bucket of sorrow spill without anyone trying to fix it or to fill it back up with well-meaning words. Sometimes we need to allow ourselves to feel the empty spaces left by the loss of our loved ones. At these times, the last thing we may want is comfort—at the least the kind that seeks to mute our grief.

When the storm had passed and my sobs had subsided, the air felt still around me. The continuous *whoosh* of the tires on the road was like a lullaby, rocking me back to the present moment in the cradle of my car. The image of Dad was still there in my mind, but it was different now. Letting go of some of my sadness had perhaps cleared my vision, freeing me to see something beyond the pain of his absence. Now when I pictured him, I saw more than the man I had known as a father: I felt I was glimpsing something of his essential spirit. He was there, with his deep-brown eyes and knowing smile, but he was also radiating profound wisdom and love. I was overwhelmed with gratitude, and I flung my thanks into the heavens as far as I could, like a shout that echoes beyond one's ability to follow it.

I drove in silence staring straight ahead for miles and miles, my right hand resting on the gearshift while steering with my left. That's when it happened. I began to feel my dad's hand resting lightly on mine. Or, to put it more accurately, I became aware of it, as if it had been there all along. It was his gentle touch, his warmth, his unmistakable comfort. "Dad," I whispered into the silence. I was afraid to move or to breathe, and I dared not look to my right at the passenger's seat. I didn't have to—I could feel him there. I could feel his hand enveloping mine, could picture his nails and the shape of his fingers. My heart leapt but I didn't flinch. Instead, I soaked in the sensation of his hand on mine. I felt he was there to comfort and reassure me of all we had discussed over the years: namely, that death is but a doorway to another life, and this life is wonderful. Eventually, the feel of his hand dissipated, as I knew it would. But I was left marveling at the experience.

There are those who think and believe differently when it comes to the unexplainable. I can speak only to what has been shared with me and what I have found true and comforting myself. When Jesus was transfigured before a few of his friends, joined by Moses and Elijah, he punctured our flimsy constructs about what is possible and what is permitted. Life goes on after death, of this I am certain. If Moses and Elijah could appear solidly enough for the disciples to suggest pitching tents for them, why wouldn't it be possible to feel my dad's hand on mine? We know so little and yet we fear so much.

Some of us are haunted by the past, by things we said or failed to say, by things we wish we could have done differently, and by memories that still make us shudder. The mournful wailing of these inner ghosts can reverberate for years in the quiet chambers of our hearts. They disturb our sleep and make us chase after *what if*s in an endless circle, like a dog that cannot catch its tail. These metaphorical ghosts are both a distraction and a torture. They keep us from living in the present, weighing us down with all that cannot be changed, while taunting us with the uncertainty of what we might have done differently. When we are frozen by fear or haunted by the past, we can become ghosts of ourselves.

As human beings who grieve and as spiritual beings who yearn for connection, we can feel stuck between two worlds. Whether trying to make peace with the past or contact with the departed, we sometimes stand frozen in the crossroads. What we yearn for the most is, unfortunately, that which can never be achieved in this lifetime: to reverse what has happened (death) and to have our loved ones with us again. The only bridge between these two realities is love. With love, we can forgive ourselves for all the *what if*s, we can forgive our loved ones for leaving us, and we can begin the movement toward acceptance and peace. With love, there is hope, and with hope, faith, and with faith, the promise of heaven, which is where our loved ones reside. And it is there where we will meet them.

Meditation: Today I will try to remember that my loved ones' lives are ongoing and did not cease with death. Even though I cannot see them, I will trust that they are there.

Affirmation: I open myself in faith to all I cannot see.

> My Father's house has many rooms; if that
> were not so, would I have told you that I am
> going there to prepare a place for you?
>
> —John 14:2

Home

There is no quiet like that after the death of someone you love. Whether this person has died at home or in a hospital setting, the world is suddenly muted, as if the last heartbeat took all the sound with it. Almost immediately, one becomes acutely aware of the irreversible aftermath of loss, including the strangeness of what was once most familiar—the home. The adjustment can be terribly difficult. Whether we want to or not, we must face the challenge of living in our homes without that beloved presence or the sweet voice on the other end of the phone.

Each room is like a rose, with its own particular beauty and painful thorns. For those who have lost their life's partner, the bedroom can be the epicenter of absence. It speaks of intimacy, both emotional and physical. It is where late-night whispers and early-morning conversations have taken place. It is where dreams have mingled, legs have entwined, and comfort was as close as the hand you could touch in the darkness. Even when someone has been in the hospital or a nursing facility for a lengthy period of time, the remnants of presence remain, leading part of us to believe that as long as our loved one is alive, he or she could come home. And so we hold the empty space in bed, as if saving a seat for our beloved. Maybe he will be there soon. Maybe she has just been delayed. We cope by hoping for their return, even if the chances are slim. With death, however, comes the finality of loss. We are no longer placeholders. The bed suddenly feels too big, and there is no question about whose side is whose. Faced with this unchangeable reality, some choose to stay on their side, while others move to the middle in search of any traces of breath or fragments of dreams that may still be lingering.

The bedroom of a child who has died can become a sanctuary or a torture chamber—sometimes it functions as both. A mother might lie on the bed, searching for the faintest scent of her child's presence. A father might sit in the corner, absorbing the things that were cherished by his daughter or important to his son. The hunger to draw a child close again may prompt a search for clues, as if the outcome might be different if we could only understand the mystery of their absence. There is an understandable hunger to collect as much of them as possible in the things that they touched, in what they loved, and in who they were. The decision to keep the bedroom intact or to change it is an individual one, but the pain is universal and unavoidable.

Sometimes homes need to be cleaned out when a loved one dies, although they can feel empty before a single piece of furniture is moved. The presence of love is what makes a home. When love is gone, all that remains is the house. The sifting and sorting that must be done can trigger memories, both beautiful and painful. It can be hard to let go of the talismans that have been collected over the years. Moving signifies closing a chapter and can magnify the sense of loss. In the midst of this, it's important to remember that what has already been can never be taken from us. The past is, perhaps, the only sure thing we have. It is inked on the pages of our lives, not penciled in. And there is some comfort in that.

The home I grew up in as a child was leveled to widen the road many years ago. When my parents told me this was happening, I was devastated, even though they were no longer living there and I was married and living in another part of the country. Most of my childhood memories were in that house. My bedroom with its view of the moon and my favorite tree, the kitchen where my mother cooked endless meals, the basement where my sisters and brothers and I played—all of this was going to be destroyed. I would never be able to drive past the house with my children and say, "This is where I grew up."

I wanted to save a brick, a stone, something tangible from that place. I thought I needed it to hold on to those memories. As the years go by, however, I find this isn't necessary; the house is intact in my mind. When I shut my eyes, I can visit each room. I can still see the living room wallpaper, the bell near the kitchen window that Mom would ring to call us for dinner, the giant neon sun my sister painted on her bedroom wall, the poster of Hemingway in my dad's study that we were convinced turned into a werewolf in the dark. It is all still there.

As my mom prepares to move, this time from the last house where she and Dad lived together, she struggles with the fear of leaving him behind. "I know he will come with me," she says. But a part of her is unconvinced. Will she be leaving him in the hologram of his favorite chair, his place at the table, his desk downstairs? Does his exhalation still linger in the air, even though it's been over two years since his death? In her sadness, she forgets it was never this or any house that was home for him. It was always her.

When people who are dying say they want to go home, I'm pretty sure they are not yearning for a particular place but rather that feeling of belonging and deep love. This can be confusing for family members who might be standing at their bedsides. What does it mean for loved ones who are dying in a hospital or nursing facility? Does it mean they should be moved? For those in their own homes, does it mean they are confused?

Yearning for home, especially when one's time here on earth is growing short, may tell us something about heaven. The homes we create with a life partner, a family, a best friend are unique. They have their own personalities, their own quirks, their own colors and textures and traditions and inside jokes. They should be the place where we feel most ourselves, most loved, and most at ease. Jesus said heaven is a lot like that—there is a room for all of us, and we will feel at home there.

Perhaps the dying process activates an instinctual turn toward our origin and the experience of complete connection. The first home any of us inhabited was the womb, a place specifically designed for us, one where we received everything we needed and more. Life requires us to outgrow that place, but our cells remember, our spirits remember. And so we try to re-create this heaven for ourselves and for one another by fashioning a home here on earth. Deep down, we know that it is temporary, that we cannot live here forever. But it is still painful when someone leaves us for the real deal. We should be happy for our loved ones, and sometimes we are, but the rooms feel so empty without them.

Maybe the best we can do is to wish our loved ones well. They have not abandoned us; they have not moved out. They are merely going ahead of us. The love they have known will be the constellation by which they will set their course. Even as we continue to search for them in the rooms of our houses and our hearts, we can trust that they are Home—and we will find them waiting there.

Meditation: Today I will imagine my departed loved ones completely happy and at home in that place lovingly prepared for them. I will wish them well and trust that—one day—we will be together again.

Affirmation: My heart is a home that is never empty. It is filled with love, and I will keep the door open.

So many people are shut up tight inside themselves like boxes, yet they would open up, unfolding quite wonderfully, if only you were interested in them.

—Sylvia Plath, "Initiation"

Isolation

I balanced the large pot of carrot soup rather precariously on my knee and reached for the doorbell. It was still warm from the stove, but its earthy aroma was contained beneath the heavy lid. As I waited for the door to open, thoughts both large and small ran through my mind. *I wish I had added more salt. Is it dumb to bring soup? I don't really know this woman very well. What a terrible loss.* Even though the pot I was holding was substantial, I still felt empty handed. What can one bring to a family, to a mother, whose ten-month-old baby has just died of SIDS?[*]

The door opened and a petite, older woman greeted me. Her expression was drawn but her eyes were clear, and there was a strength in her face that was rather formidable. She was the baby's grandmother, the mother's mother. I introduced myself, offering my condolences

---

[*] Sudden infant death syndrome.

(and my soup) and awkwardly admitting that I had only the beginnings of a friendship with her daughter. I told her how we had met two years earlier in a playgroup for our firstborns, our daughters, who were a year apart—a group, it turns out, that neither of us had subsequently attended. When we discovered this upon our next chance meeting, we laughed, and the seeds of our friendship were planted. By then, we both had infant sons, mine being two months older than hers. We exchanged phone numbers while standing on the street and promised to get together soon.

The days might be long but the weeks pass quickly when you are a mother of two young children. I was not surprised, then, when several months passed before I saw her again. It was on the same street in our little town, where every shop owner is known by name and they, in turn, know you and your children's names. I smiled when I saw her, but the expression was ripped from my face with the brute speed and force of a cobra. "My baby died" were the words that shot from her mouth before I could even say her name. *What? What?* I could have sworn the ground trembled, and I felt the need to hold on to something before an earthquake split the sidewalk apart. In that moment, I suppose it had. What I didn't realize, what I *couldn't* have realized then, was that a fault line had been formed. It could have left her standing on one side, with the terrible loss of her son, and me on the other, but miraculously it didn't. Perhaps, in that moment, we had simultaneously reached for each other, forming a durable bridge of shared love and pain.

Standing on the doorstep with my soup was the first time I had ever been to her home. I had yet to learn that my new friend was a

gourmet cook and that this would be the only time I would ever prepare food for her. Her mother thanked me for coming but said that
her daughter was resting. She took the pot from my hands, placing it
just inside the entryway. Then she closed the door and joined me on
the front step. We stood there quietly for a moment, looking at the
ground, at the sky, at each other, and blinking back the tears. Neither
of us let them fall, even though a storm was clearly coming. Just as I
was about to turn and leave, her mother's gaze held me in place. "You
know," she began, "my daughter doesn't really need you now. She has
lots of family around her. But she will need you tomorrow and the
next day and the day after that. She will need you after her family has
gone home and everyone else is afraid to come. Will you be that
friend?"

What she clearly knew, and what I had yet to understand, is that
death can create a lonely fortress for the living. It's hard to emerge
from our places of sorrow when we are raw and vulnerable and shattered. What makes this even more isolating is that very few people
seem to want to come in, at least after the initial news of our loss. It's
as if grief has carved out a terrifying moat that keeps others at bay.
Only those who are willing to cross that chasm, unarmed, into another's sorrow will be welcomed, even if a part of them is afraid.

I was afraid—mostly of intruding—but my friend's mother had
asked me to do just that. And so I did. I began to call or visit her every
day. We shared countless meals together (that she cooked and I enjoyed), and we shared our lives. At first I was afraid that the sight of
my son, who bore an uncanny resemblance to hers, would be too upsetting for her. But she embraced and loved him. In the years that

followed, my son would stand, in some ways, as a marker for hers. She could imagine where her son would have been developmentally. We celebrated milestones together. As the years passed, our girls became friends, our lives became entwined, and eventually the painful genesis of our friendship became interwoven with shared experiences of laughter and joy. Sometimes all we need to keep from falling into despair is a hand that is reaching for us. But we must also be willing to reach for it.

Isolation can set in when people stop knocking at the door and we stop wanting them to knock. The desire to curl into a little ball when we are grief stricken is understandable, but staying there for too long is dangerous. We have a responsibility to our own souls to live. We cannot honor those we have lost by wasting what they no longer have—life. No matter how good my intentions, nothing would have been gained had my friend not opened the door of her heart to me, had she not taken my calls or allowed me to visit.

Although it seems unfair, people often look to the bereaved for clues about how to cross the bridge into their fortress of pain. Some fear saying the wrong thing, so they don't say anything at all. They avoid. Some can become impatient with another's sadness. They want their friend or loved one to be "back to normal," which also means *they* want to be back to normal. If you are the one grieving, your friends might say that they miss who you were before your life was wrecked by loss. When it becomes clear they cannot fix you, an irrational anger can begin to fester in those who are on the periphery of your sorrow. How long is long enough when it comes to grieving?

Because there is no algorithm for grief, and no road map, it's hard to know what to expect on the journey. One would think we'd be better navigators since it's virtually impossible to go through life without experiencing the death of someone we love. Perhaps it's because grief is a singular experience. We mourn differently because we love differently. We can feel alone, even when siblings, friends, or a loved one shares our pain, because every relationship is unique. Perhaps the best we can do is to stay connected to one another, love one another, brave the moats of sorrow, and show up without an agenda. When you have a friend who is grieving, remember to keep knocking. When you are the bereaved, be willing to open the door.

Meditation: Today I will reach for the hand of a friend when I am feeling most isolated, and I will be a friend to someone who is hurting.

Affirmation: Even in sorrow, I am connected to others. I need not suffer alone.

> The pain of parting is nothing to the joy
> of meeting again.
>
> —Charles Dickens, *Nicholas Nickleby*

Joy

"Will I ever be happy again?" she asked. The woman looking up at me had lost her husband of fifty years. Although they had three grown children who were very attentive and caring, she still felt alone. Her husband had been her life and she had been his, especially since their children had married and started families of their own. She explained that everything she cared about, and almost every happy moment, revolved around him and their life together. Her entire life was viewed through that lens. Her husband's departure had been swift and unexpected; she didn't even have the chance to say good-bye. Now, sitting across the table from me, she looked small and vulnerable. "What am I going to do?" she asked. "How am I going to live?" I don't think she was expecting an answer; she just needed to give voice to her pain. This was not something that I, nor anyone else for that matter, could fix. One cannot forcibly infuse joy or meaning into another person. It is something ignited and experienced only in relationship—with another person, with nature, with animals, with God. Joy is our birthright. Though its flame can be dimmed and even doused by circumstance, it can also be rekindled. But it is up to us to strike the match.

Beneath the surface of every interaction and every moment is the reality of loss for those who are grieving. Whether sitting in church, going to the grocery store, chatting with a friend, or holding a child, it's not unusual to feel emotionally split, as if living a dual reality. How we are functioning on the outside is often not reflective of what is happening on the inside. If we could photograph this, it might look like a double exposure. Grief is a layer that we wear on our hearts and spirits, at least for a time. Initially, it might be like outerwear. We wrap ourselves in it—we may even lose ourselves in it—and others understand that we cannot take it off in their presence, even if we tried. When it becomes too heavy or uncomfortable to lug around, we tuck it under the surface of our skin or pack it away in an interior closet. But we never forget it is there.

Grief takes up so much space that it can leave little room for joy. After a significant loss, many feel as if they literally need to learn how to be happy again. It's like learning how to live without a part of oneself. Perhaps the first step is finding the courage to *want* to be happy. Sometimes we are afraid to allow ourselves to feel joyful. We hold on to the sharp edges of our grief, as if pain is what tethers our loved ones to us. If we feel happy, does it mean we have let them go? It can already seem as if they have slipped through our fingers, as if their dear presence has eluded our grasp. No wonder most of us are afraid of letting go, even of pain. We do not want to relax our grip because we fear more will be taken from us. Perhaps we also cling to our pain because it is the last thing we experienced in relationship to our loved ones. And so we guard it. It is like a room we keep to remind ourselves (and others) that they lived. But the pain of grief is rooted in separation, and so that room will always be empty. The only thing that can fill it is joy. And joy springs from knowing we are always connected to those we love. Professor Joseph Campbell famously suggested that we "find a place inside where there's joy, and the joy will burn out the pain." Allowing ourselves to feel joyful, or at least opening ourselves to the possibility of joy, sets us in the right direction. If we want to bring our loved ones closer—spiritually, emotionally, or metaphorically—we must give ourselves permission to be happy.

Happiness is difficult when you are grieving, not just because it can be elusive, but also because of how it may be perceived by others. One man told me he was afraid to appear happy in public. "If I have one small moment of laughing with a friend," he said, "and someone sees me, they think that I am over my wife's death. But this could not be further from the truth." Another woman, who had recently lost her fiancé, shared what happened when she was with some colleagues. They had attended a wake for a coworker's elderly mother. Although this was hard for her to do, having just lost her beloved, she felt it was important to support her friend. Afterward, when she and her coworkers stopped to get a bite to eat, someone suggested taking a photo since they were rarely all together. The next day, a colleague casually remarked that the woman must be feeling much better since she was smiling in the picture. "What was I supposed to do," she asked, "ruin the picture by making a sad face?" Even though it had been hard for her to smile, she did so because she didn't want to draw attention to herself. Many who are grieving express the same concern: If they appear happy, will others forget that their hearts are broken?

Perhaps this is why some continue to wear their wedding or engagement rings for a time—even for life—following the deaths of their beloveds. This outward expression of an inward pain is a constant reminder to others that they have lost someone they love. In a sense, it's like a flashing sign that says, "I am still Mrs. So-and-so." That's one of the problems with letting go of our grief: it can feel as if we are also letting go of an essential part of who we are. If we are happy, even for a moment, do we cease to be someone's wife, someone's husband, someone's mother, someone's friend? Will other people forget that our loved ones existed?

When the topic of happiness comes up in a bereavement group, I often ask people what they think their loved ones would say to them, if they could, and what they would want for them. Almost invariably, the answer is "He would want me to be happy" or "My son would say, 'Mom, don't cry'" or "She would say, 'You did a great job caring for me.'" And when I ask them to imagine what they would say to their loved ones if the roles were reversed, if it was they who had died instead, the atmosphere in the room changes. It becomes lighter, softer. The eyes of those gathered become clearer and stronger. "I would not want my loved one to be sad." "I would want him to go on with his life and be happy." "I would want her to find joy." These are the responses. The theologian Karl Barth said, "Joy is the simplest form of gratitude." If we can access our gratitude for having known and loved those we have lost, perhaps we can begin again to experience joy.

Meditation: Today I will try to be happy for some part of the day. I will not be afraid to let go of my pain, and I will not be concerned about how I am perceived.

Affirmation: With a grateful heart, I open myself to joy.

We bereaved are not alone. We belong to
the largest company in all the world—the
company of those who have known suffering.

—Helen Keller

Kinship

As social creatures, we seek connection with other human beings. Aside from family ties, what draws us together can be anything from our particular stage in life to similar beliefs, a shared interest, or a common purpose. Sometimes what connects us is a spontaneous sense of trust, a gut feeling of mutual understanding upon which a friendship begins to form. Usually the things we share are those that we have consciously chosen. We have kids, so we easily relate to other parents. We've chosen to get a dog, putting us in the company of other dog owners. We've joined a house of worship corresponding with our beliefs. We play tennis, we fight for the environment, we are musicians. When we encounter a person with whom we share something in common, especially something that is essential to our spirits, the heart opens. This is the experience of kinship. Kinship is the bond that is formed not necessarily by blood but by a deep empathy because of what is held in common.

There is also an accidental kinship that happens among people who have experienced a similar trauma or circumstance. The tie that binds them could be that they are coping with a child with special needs or have a parent or life partner with Alzheimer's. It could be that they have survived a disaster, such as an earthquake or, God forbid, a terrorist attack. Kinship is also found among those who are in recovery from an addiction or an illness. Women newly diagnosed with breast cancer, for example, often feel a sense of community with other women who have suffered and survived this diagnosis and treatment. I've heard women say, "Being a breast cancer survivor is a club you don't want to be in, but you meet the greatest women." Clearly, there are experiences that one would rather not have, but the path is more bearable when traveling it with a friend.

Grief is like this in some ways. We have little to no control over what happens to our loved ones. We cannot prevent them from getting ill, from having an accident, from overdosing, from committing suicide. And when the other shoe drops, we are thrust into the company of the bereaved. It may feel like being washed overboard and suddenly finding ourselves thrashing about in dangerous waters. If we look around, we will surely see others who are struggling to stay afloat. Obviously, everyone would rather be on the boat, but it's less terrifying knowing that we are not alone and that countless others have braved these same waters. We don't want to be there. But at some point in our lives all of us will be—if we have dared to love.

In the most painful situations, I have seen the healing power of kinship. And part of the balm it offers is the feeling of being fully understood, without having to explain anything. When words *are* shared, it's like they are being collected and gently held in a communal basket along with the broken hearts of the listeners, especially when there is a similar loss. Parents who have lost a child, for example, usually feel more understood in the company of other bereaved parents. They have all experienced the unfathomable, and the challenges they face going forward are painfully relatable. In the same way, people who have lost a spouse can often find comfort among other widows and widowers because they, too, know what it's like to face their days without their life's partner. Sharing the pain of loss with those who can personally relate to you does not make the pain go away, but it makes it less lonely.

I found this several years ago in the eyes of a man whose sister had died. While planning her memorial service, we discovered that we had both worked at Ground Zero after September 11, he as a firefighter and I as a chaplain. Each year as that anniversary comes around, we don't need to say a word. I can see it in his eyes, he can see it in mine—the aftermath of a trauma that will always be there, the scars of heartbreak. While I wouldn't have wished this experience on him, I am grateful for the kinship we share and the comfort of knowing that someone else has an inkling of how I might be feeling. I imagine it is the same for victims of, or first responders to, other horrific events such as the school and workplace shootings that occur too often these days, tearing the country and the globe apart. The love and support of people on the outside of a trauma are crucial, but the bond that is shared by those who have experienced it is kinship.

Losing a loved one is so painful, but you need not suffer alone.

Just outside your door are others who are grieving or have grieved. Guaranteed. At first you may not want to identify with them. You may even distance yourself from them because you don't want to *be* them. This, however, will not make the death of your loved one less real. I knew a woman who, soon after losing her husband, avoided other widows. She didn't want to be one of *them*. Although, individually, some of these women were her friends, she didn't want to be part of a group that she had no choice in joining. As the reality of her husband's death set in, however, she softened in her feelings toward them. She allowed herself the comfort of their company and found meaning in the gentle flow of support. Her pain did not increase when she was with these women; instead, it was a fraction less.

When we allow ourselves to connect on a deeper level with others who are missing and grieving loved ones—whether their loss is similar to ours or not—we open ourselves up to the comfort of kinship. In doing so, the world feels a little less foreign and we feel less like a stranger in it. Remembering that we are part of a global family, that death does not discriminate and that we will *all* know the pain of loss, will not bring our loved ones back, but it tethers us to each other. It helps us comfort each other. "What we have once enjoyed we can never lose," wrote Helen Keller. "All that we love deeply becomes a part of us." Her words, like pieces of driftwood, are there to help you hold your head above water until you can make it to shore. And the ones paddling along with you, as well as those who are waiting with a warm embrace, will most likely be the sisters and brothers who belong to the company of the bereaved.

Meditation: Today I will not close myself off to others who are grieving. I will envision myself as part of a community: one people, one family, created to love and care for each other.

Affirmation: As part of a global family, I am never alone in my grief.

Where you used to be, there is a hole in the world, which I find myself constantly walking around in the daytime, and falling in at night.

—Edna St. Vincent Millay

Loneliness

Of all the challenges that come with losing someone, loneliness can be the most devastating and difficult to overcome. This is true not only for those who have lost their precious life's partner but also for those who have lost a soul's companion, such as a best friend or a sibling. Those who find themselves living alone for the first time in years can feel trapped by silence, the same silence that was once enjoyed because it was shared with a loved one. After a death, it can become oppressive. But even those who were not living with or even near a loved one can feel lonely. Having a friend in the world who truly understands us and whom we understand, who loves us and whom we love, can make the world less lonely. These deep relationships connect us, not only to one another, but also to ourselves and to the greater community. One's identity as part of a couple or a family or a friendship is often the lens through which the world is seen and understood. The hand we yearn to hold is usually that which steadies and comforts us or which solicits our deep desire to comfort. But what happens when this person is gone? When we want to reflect on a memory or share something that has just happened to us, when we want to comment on the news or giggle at an inside joke, the absence of our loved ones can send us tumbling into despair. One does not have to live alone to feel lonely, but being alone compounds the reality of loss.

Loneliness can settle in like darkness on the brightest day, as if death itself has eclipsed the sun at noon. It can feel like a prison, unavoidable, unchangeable, a life sentence of emotional and spiritual solitary confinement. If left unattended, it becomes a whirlpool of sorts, pulling everything inward in tighter and tighter concentric circles until we are drowning in it. Because death is unfixable, something that cannot be undone, many surrender to loneliness as if that, too, can never change, as if they are powerless to weaken its course.

I have thought a lot about loneliness. Whether anticipating the loss of those I hold closest to my heart or listening to others share during a bereavement group, I, too, have shuddered in the face of its terrible shadow. "I am so lonely." These are the words that often render me speechless. What can be said in the face of this truth? There are no real strategies I can give, none that would address the deep-down despair of it all. When the only sufficient antidote to pain would be the sudden appearance of a loved one in a miraculous reversal of death, words fall short. As a person of faith, however, I cannot believe we are meant to live our lives in this way. I cannot believe God would leave us in the vortex of despair without a rope to grab on to. Perhaps the real challenge is mustering the desire to reach for it. "Why should I stay at the bottom of a well / when a strong rope is in my hand?" asked

Rumi, the thirteenth-century poet and mystic.* Why? Because sometimes we are afraid that grabbing it will mean moving on.

The rope God throws doesn't come just once; it comes over and over and over again. It comes disguised as the telephone, which can be both answered and dialed when we need to talk to someone. Instead of waiting for a call, we can call someone to talk. In the words of Fred Rogers, "It takes strength to face our sadness and to grieve and to let our grief and our anger flow in tears when they need to. It takes strength to talk about our feelings and to reach out for help and comfort when we need it."† Picking up the phone is one way to grab on to the rope. God's rope also comes in the form of happy memories. When we allow ourselves to feel grateful for having known our loved ones and for the sweet memories we have of them, we are reaching for the rope God has thrown us. We can also reach for God's help when we reach out to others who may be hurting. This necessitates holding the rope with one hand while tossing it to someone else with the other. Chances are, someone ahead has done the same thing for you. Maybe the best way to reach for God is to reach for one another. The rope God throws can come as music, as prayer, as creativity. The rope is a lifeline that connects us to our Source and reminds us that we are never truly alone. We are connected, always connected, to God, to each other, and to our loved ones.

A ninety-nine-year-old woman who had been married for seventy-

---

* Jonathan Star, trans., *Rumi: In the Arms of the Beloved* (New York: Jeremy P. Tarcher/ Putnam, 1997), 124.

† Fred Rogers, *The World According to Mr. Rogers: Important Things to Remember* (New York: Hyperion, 2003), 15.

six years taught me about coping with loneliness. Although she had adult children, she had outlived her friends, her pets, and finally her husband. Was she lonely? Sometimes. Was she despairing? No. When I asked how she coped with her husband's absence, she told me that she savored the happy times they had shared. "I talk to Tom," she said, her eyes glistening. "I can't see him but I know he's there. I especially feel him beside me in the morning, before I even open my eyes." She also invoked the comfort of his presence by reading the poetry that he used to recite to her every night before bed. She didn't know the poems by heart, the way he had, but she knew *him* by heart. She felt him in each word and could hear his voice. What's more, by sharing these poems with others, she felt the nearness of his presence. Her favorite was one about a spider, written by E. B. White. Observing the rise and fall of the spider as she constructs her web, the narrator notices that a ladder is also being built to the place where the spider started. The narrator then uses this metaphor to reassure his loved one that although he is going away, he will "Attach one silken strand to you / For my returning."*

That strand, as strong as spider's silk, was the rope she held on to. She had no doubt that he would come for her one day and that they would be together. In fact, she died less than nine months after her husband.

Loneliness isn't something you can talk yourself out of. Passive waiting won't lift it, and you can't outrun it. Easing the weight of it seems to necessitate some sort of action, including, first and foremost,

---

* E. B. White, *Letters of E. B. White,* ed. Dorothy Lobrano Guth, rev. ed., ed. Martha White (New York: HarperCollins, 2006), 88–89.

a shift in perspective, a willingness to feel differently. This can be scary, especially when being lonely reminds us and others of all we have lost. The internal movement toward comfort, toward God, toward the recognition that we are *not* alone, can be as subtle as the slightest upward tilt of the chin. That's all we need. That in itself is a prayer and an invitation to allow the light in again. We are not powerless over the feeling of loneliness. We can choose to feel better—or at least to *want* to feel better. Finding ways to share about our loved ones with others is one way to invite them in. Participating in the things they enjoyed is another way to infuse activities with their presence. Trusting that life does not end here and opening ourselves to the promise of reunion lights a candle in the darkness of despair. With each anecdote lovingly recounted, we bring them closer. With each loving action, we can feel their warmth. With each leap of faith, we shorten the distance between them and us. If we focus only on the unchangeable—the absence of those we love most—loneliness may threaten to undo us. What we *can* change, however, is our awareness of the myriad ways they—and God—manifest themselves to us.

Frederick Buechner suggested that "to be lonely is to be aware of an emptiness which it takes more than people to fill. It is to sense that something is missing which you cannot name."* That missing something, he went on to ponder, is more even than your dearest loved one. On a deeper level, we are lonely for "the place we know best by longing for it, where at last we become who we are, where finally we find

---

* Frederick Buechner, *Whistling in the Dark: A Doubter's Dictionary* (New York: HarperCollins, 1988), 83.

home."* This place is our spiritual origin, that from which we came. It is complete union with the Divine, which some call heaven. Loving someone deeply brings a bit of that heaven to earth. Perhaps we are less lonely when they are here because they remind us of who we are in relation to who God is. The love we share warms our hearts and ignites our spirits. When they die, it's like they have rolled out of bed, taking the covers with them. We feel a chill. We reach for them in the darkness. God does not leave us alone and shivering in the cold, even though for a time our hearts may tell us differently. Love never lets go of our hands. Never. We came into the world as individual souls— held, blessed, named, loved—and we have a responsibility to our souls to keep living, living until we make our own way back home. Those who have gone before us have left torches along the path in the form of lessons imparted, examples set, and people who need our help. When we are willing to embark again on the path, to grab on to whatever rope God throws us in our times of loneliness and despair, our loved ones will be there to guide us.

Meditation: Today I will reach for the rope God is throwing me to ease my loneliness. And with the other hand, I will reach for someone else who is lonely.

Affirmation: Loneliness cannot overwhelm me when I stay connected to God.

---

* Buechner, *Whistling in the Dark,* 83.

If all you can do is crawl, start crawling.

—Rumi

Moving On

How long do we get to mourn? Depends on who you ask. The standard answer from employers is three to five business days—about the length of time it takes to get a package delivered. If you can't deliver yourself back to work in that time, then there's obviously a problem. How long do we get to mourn? Most friends and associates will grant us about thirty days; then the expectation is that one "gets back to normal." How long do we get to mourn? Almost always less time than we need, or can admit to needing, before being expected to move on. The reality is, with the exception of those closest to us, others around us *have* moved on and, by implication, so should we. Sadness is inconvenient and uncomfortable for those on the perimeter of grief. It's understandable in the beginning, but not if it goes on too long. Who, however, determines how long is long enough?

It's a strange thing to admit that we are uncomfortable with grief even though all of us have, or will have, suffered it at some point. If one is perceived as lingering too long in sorrow, others recoil. If one is seen smiling or, God forbid, laughing in public after a loss, others may respond critically, as in, "It sure didn't take *that* lady long to get over her husband's death!" How and when do we move on from the death of someone we love? Can we move on? And what would this look like if we did?

The forward movement of time is something over which we have no control. When we are grieving, it may feel as if we are being dragged along, despite our resistance. Even if we try to dig our nails into the last lingering moments shared with our loved ones, they will slip from our fingers and begin to recede into the past. This can be very scary. We are forced to move forward in time, but it doesn't mean we are moving on emotionally. The heart has its own time. It is a clock that runs at a different pace. It can't be rushed or set ahead an hour. It doesn't ring like an alarm, signaling that it's time to get on with things. We cannot be woken from or wedged out of our grief, but we can begin to ease ourselves into the flow of life again.

The donning of black clothes in response to death used to be a way for mourners to let others know where their hearts stood. In many communities, it still functions as an outward sign of what is happening internally. How long it is worn varies, but the message is basically the same: "I am grieving. Don't ask me to do otherwise." Except for the funeral service, many of us no longer utilize that black billboard of sorrow. And so we have to find ways to let others know that we are still in the throes of grief, that we are not ready to resume normal life, and, perhaps most importantly, that we want our loss to be remembered. We want our loved ones to be remembered. Even as we begin to move on from the epicenter of our pain, from the moment our loved ones left us, we want to plant our feet in what was. When we are perceived as "getting better" and "moving forward," people around us may breathe a sigh of relief. But for the grieving, these terms can imply a letting go of loved ones that many are not yet prepared to do.

I am reminded of a twenty-six-year-old woman who told me of standing at the coffin of her young husband. He had been diagnosed with a rare lung cancer a few months after she found out she was pregnant with their son. He died three days after the baby's first birthday. At his wake someone remarked, with good intentions I'm sure, "Don't worry, sweetheart. You are so young and pretty—I'm sure you will find someone."

"I did find someone," she replied. "He's right there, lying in that coffin."

Moving on, whatever that entails, is not possible if one does not stop to grieve, and grieve deeply in proportion to the loss. There are no quick fixes to heartbreak. The young widow knew this, and she bravely set her own course, at her own pace, for both her and her son.

In the end, "moving on" is rarely a term used by the bereaved. More often than not it's used by concerned loved ones who want to help or by acquaintances who are uncomfortable with death. No one wants to see his or her friend, mother, father, or beloved suffer for a prolonged period of time. Those who are grieving the death of a loved one intuitively know they are not meant to stay entrenched in the deepest part of their pain. They are not meant to live in the past. Eventually, they must decide to live again, but no one can decide for them.

Perhaps the term "moving on" could be replaced with the concept of "living on." For that is what we are called to do: to live on, despite the pain of our losses. Moving on implies that we are leaving something behind, that we have closed a chapter, like closing and locking a house. But we don't leave our loved ones in the rearview mirror. We don't leave them in the ground or scattered in the sea—we take them with us. We take the times we have shared and the love we still feel into whatever future awaits us. We don't move on; we move *with.* Our spirits are embroidered with silver threads stitching us to our loved ones. They are adorned with the jewels of every moment shared and all that we cherished about them. By our choosing to live on, they can live on. If we dissolve into the darkness of despair, they cannot shine. Our loved ones do not want us to stop living because they have died; they want us to live. They want us to bring them with us into each new day so that a part of them can remain on earth through the stories we share. After a time, however long that is (and it is different for different people), sorrow ceases to be a tribute to the deceased. It distracts from *their* stories and puts the focus on *us,* on our pain, on our lives. They have not moved on from us; they are living within and beyond us. And we have not moved on from them when we take a step toward happiness, acceptance, and peace. We live on together when we live on in love.

Meditation: Today I will try to take a baby step from my sorrow toward a future that includes happiness. I will choose to live on, knowing that my loved one is living on with me.

Affirmation: I carry my loved one wherever I go.

Though my soul may set in darkness, it
will rise in perfect light;
I have loved the stars too fondly to be
fearful of the night.

—Sarah Williams

Night

When night begins to fall, so do the spirits of many who are grieving. The busyness that often provides welcome distraction during the day must now be set aside. The phone stops ringing, the television goes off. Family members, whether living at home or somewhere else, prepare for bed. And the lights will soon go out. In the wintertime, depending on where one lives, night comes sooner and lasts longer. It stretches out its velvet blanket and tucks in the sun before either of us is ready to retire. The hours can be long as we wait for the sun to wake, like a toddler tumbling out of her bed of sky.

There is no getting around night. It's part of our day-to-days, so to speak. But we can, perhaps, better prepare for it so that it does not become an inescapable torture, something we dread rather than welcome. With night comes quiet, and quiet sometimes leads to a small room within ourselves that we find hard to escape. We feel around the padded walls of it, hoping for a secret passageway out, where death has not touched us and where our loved ones must be waiting. We can feel trapped by Night and by its henchman, Quiet. They hold us hostage, with nothing to do but chase the *what if*s and the *what now*s in our minds. Night brings the reality of the empty space in the bed, the empty room down the hall. It can open the floodgate to images we've managed to keep at bay during the day, images that are now projected onto the ceiling in the dark. Thus, many lie awake, counting the hours until morning.

What we forget is that night also offers a unique gift: the chance to meet our loved ones as we dream. In dreams, we can see and hear and touch them again. In dreams, for a few flickering moments, there is no separation of worlds. Our loved ones can be with us in a way that is impossible when we are awake. We can talk with them, we can look into their eyes, we can ask them questions. Night not only offers us a chance to rest—because grief is exhausting—but also allows the heart some time to recharge.

The topic of dreaming often comes up with the bereaved. Some people are able to recount vivid dreams of being with their beloved ones; others yearn for such an experience. After listening to group members share about their dreams, one woman asked, "Why won't my husband come to *me* in a dream?" She was upset that she had never had a "visitation" similar to what others seemed to have had. She yearned for the experience of being with her husband again, if only in a dream. I hesitated before addressing her concern. I didn't want to set her up for more heartbreak, because there is obviously no guarantee

when it comes to dreams. Our loved ones cannot be summoned like
a movie on demand. In the daytime, we can replay and savor memories and can imagine ourselves with our loved ones, but at night, when
we are sleeping, we have no choice but to let go of the remote. Still, I
wanted to help her. "I'm curious," I said. "Have you ever *asked* your
husband to come to you in a dream? Have you ever invited him?" She
looked surprised, and I saw a small flame flicker somewhere in the far
reaches of her eyes. It was the spark of possibility. No, she told me, she
had never tried this. To be honest, neither had I. In fact, it had never
occurred to me—but I'd been inspired by something a client had
shared with me the week before.

The man, who was in his midforties, had recently lost both of
his parents, for whom he had been the primary caregiver. His
mother, in particular, had had a very difficult few months leading
up to her death. With tears in his eyes he came to me, asking not
how to invite them into his dreams but rather how to make them
stop appearing. "I can't take it much longer," he moaned. "Every
night they come. Every night they are upset with me. I can't sleep. I
dread sleep. Please help me make them stop." Red flags went up immediately, of course. Did he have things about which he felt guilty?
Was he mentally ill? I tried to offer my support while making clear
the limitations of my expertise. When he told me he was under the
care of a psychiatrist, I breathed a sigh of relief. When he said it was
the psychiatrist who had referred him to me, I had an inkling about
the complexity of his grief. Listening to his anguish, I suggested that
he simply ask his parents not to show up in his dreams anymore. He

could do this in a loving way, as in, "Mom, Dad, I need a little break," or firmly, by imagining the door to his dreams locked and guarded by an angel of his choosing. He nodded his head, wiped his bloodshot eyes, and told me he would try. The next time I saw him, he said the dreams had continued but were less intense and upsetting. It was a start anyway.

Because of this poor tortured man, it occurred to me: If we can ask loved ones to stay out of our dreams, then why not see if we can invite them in? And so I suggested this to the woman in my group. That night, ironically, I had an incredibly vivid dream about my father. I could see him very clearly. I could hear his voice and feel his presence. He looked vibrant and glowing and much healthier and younger than when he died. In short, he was restored. When I asked him how it was possible that he was there, since he had died and I had even officiated his funeral, he simply said, "I will explain everything to you one day." Then he disappeared out a door. When I went to follow him, I was stopped by an endless turquoise sea. I took a step, allowing the water to lap around my ankles, but I went no farther. I knew my dad was on the other shore. I also knew the water separating us would be impossible for me to cross. It would become too deep and too wide almost immediately. And so I stood there looking out at the water, knowing someday I would join him. It was a beautiful and powerful dream.

Others to whom I have made the suggestion have also shared their experiences. One man recently wrote me saying he had had a dream about his mother, after asking her to come to him. Danny said it was very vivid. He dreamed that he went to his parents' house. As usual, he was aware of how sad he was that his mother had died. But this time she opened the door, alive and well, just like old times. He said,

> I hugged her and kissed her and cried, thinking that I must
> have had a really bad dream, a nightmare. I was so glad that it
> wasn't true . . . I told her over and over how much I love her,
> and how I was so glad that I had been wrong and that she was
> fine. And I couldn't stop saying, "Can it really be true that my
> mom is alive and well?"

When he woke up and realized that it had been a dream, he was sad, but it was also comforting to remember how well she looked and to recall the feeling of being with her again. Reflecting on it, Danny was glad he had invited her to come to him.

If we could think of night as the time when we are potentially closest to our loved ones, not farthest from them, perhaps we would welcome sleep and allow ourselves the needed rest. Grief is exhausting. Darkness can be suffocating. But night allows us to see the stars. It offers the gift of sleep and the possibility of seeing our loved ones again in our dreams. Even if we don't see them, we still know they are there, just as the stars are there in a cloudy sky. They may be beyond our sight, they may be hidden by the bright glare of day, but they are there. If we love the stars, we must also embrace the night.

Meditation: Tonight I will allow myself to rest. I will embrace the night and the gifts it offers. I will think happy thoughts before I go to bed.

Affirmation: I welcome the night as I do the day. I open myself to dream.

> I remember the odd sensation of living in the middle of that experience and feeling, simultaneously, like it was something happening at telescopic distance. Like something I was looking at through the wrong end of a pair of binoculars.
>
> —Wally Lamb, *I Know This Much Is True*

Out of Body

Looking back over the year since her son's death, the mother explains what it was like to feel physically but not emotionally present. "I know I was functioning," she says quietly. "I got through the funeral. I consoled his friends. But *I* wasn't there, you know what I mean?" When I asked her to tell me more about this, she described the zombie-like state in which she existed for months and months after his overdose. She was understandably in shock, and shock nudged her into disassociating from what was happening within and around her. People said she was strong when, in reality, she felt like she wasn't there at all. "I was out of body," she concluded, "like this was all happening to someone else."

The shock of death, particularly a traumatic death, can practically knock us out of our own skins. Death packs a devastating punch to the living. It's like a concussion of the soul. When I was in high school, I remember hitting my head, hard, against the concrete at a track meet. While I was regaining consciousness, I became aware of other students standing around me in a circle. *What are they looking at?* I wondered. It was almost as if I had joined them in gawking at the girl who was crumpled at their feet. Only when I acknowledged that it was *I* who lay crumpled did my head begin to ache. Disassociating had spared me, momentarily, from the excruciating pain of my injury.

Similarly, in order to cope with the death of a loved one, some people seem to step out of their bodies emotionally in order to bear the reality of sorrow. It's a way of saying, to some degree or another, this terrible thing has not happened to me but to some poor soul who looks a lot like me. This type of disassociation is common among those who have suffered other traumas, such as that of sexual assault. It is a survival mechanism, one where a switch is flipped, turning some senses off in order to cope with the trauma of what is happening. Feeling out of body after a loss is the heart's way of saying, *If I allow myself to feel the full extent of this pain, I will break.*

Settling back into ourselves and into the whole truth of loss is painful. It's like reentering the atmosphere—we may have to go slowly in order to not burst into flame. But, with time, we can do just that. Honoring our sadness by eventually allowing ourselves to acknowledge the pain also helps us reintegrate into our lives. The bottom line is these *are* our lives and we *are* living them, whether half- or fully present. When we crawl back into our own skins, we may discover how strong we actually are. We can gratefully acknowledge the part of ourselves that wanted to spare the other parts such pain. We can be tender with ourselves. We may look back and wonder how we got through those first few days, weeks, months. They may be a blur. But one day we will catch our breath and see how far we have come.

"I am not out of body anymore," the mother tells me. "I am fully here. Sometimes the pain is terrible, but I'd rather feel it than pretend it's not there. When I acknowledge the reality of my son's absence, he oddly feels more real to me. After all, he came from this body of mine, and I'd rather be in it, where he once was."

Another mother told me how exercise helps her cope. "In the beginning, I was like Forrest Gump—I just started running, without knowing why. I ran and ran, probably in an effort to outrun the pain. Then it became the one way I could allow myself to be quiet. I would just focus on my breathing and will myself to keep going."

Grief is exhausting. It saps both physical and emotional energy. It keeps us awake at night and makes us listless in the day. Some find that their appetites are completely gone, while others eat for the comfort that does not come. Grief is a hunger that cannot be sated by food, but many do not know where else to turn. It can cause migraines, chest pains, anxiety, and forgetfulness; it can make the bodies we live in feel as foreign as the lives we are facing without our loved ones. There is no quick remedy for the symptoms of grief, but participating in some kind of physical activity—walking, yoga, running, stretching, swimming—may be helpful to keep from sliding into a deep depression.

Feeling out of body, or like life is surreal, is not unusual when it comes to loss. How long this might last is hard to say. Generally, one begins to integrate back into reality when the worst of the earthquake is over, the shock waves have passed, and the grief tremors are no longer a threat to survival. We settle back into our bodies when the soul intuits that it is strong enough to withstand the brute force of the reality of loss.

In the meantime, being patient and gentle with yourself is advised. Solid ground will materialize beneath your feet once more. Your outstretched hands will look like your own again, and the body you live in will begin to feel familiar. Treat it kindly! It houses the tactile memories of the one you grieve. It carries the stories that others may want to hear. It bears traces of personality, echoes of laughter, and particles of the deceased that only you can share. If we fail to show up in our lives, parts of our loved ones will be hidden. If we stop living, parts of them will be missing. When we begin to recover from our soul's concussion, the reality and the pain of loss will be felt, yes, but so will the substantial presence of our loved ones. When we have the courage to reenter our lives, we'll find our loved ones there with us.

Meditation: Today I will remember to breathe, bringing myself back into my body with each inhalation and letting go of some of my pain each time I exhale. As I reconnect my spirit to my body, I will allow myself to feel.

Affirmation: The body that I live in is strong enough to bear a broken heart.

I'll be seeing you in all the old familiar places.

—Irving Kahal, "I'll Be Seeing You"

Partings

How we leave each other matters. It matters while we are alive, and it matters even more when one of us has died. Parting can be for an hour or a lifetime. It can be as mundane as seeing your children off to school, your spouse to work, or saying good night to a friend for the evening. When we say good-bye under normal circumstances, the assumption is that we will see each other again. Hence, the partings can be hurried, they can be grouchy, they can be sweet. If we leave one another poorly, we usually get another chance to do it better the next time, to say "I'm sorry," to give one more hug, or to whisper "I love you." When we have been parted by death, we don't get that chance. We can't change the day or the manner in which our loved ones died, nor can we alter what we said or wished we'd said. Maybe we didn't get the chance to say good-bye at all. The only thing we can change is the way we think about and accept it.

During the first meeting of a new bereavement group, those who are present have an opportunity to tell a bit of their stories. They share with one another about the person they are grieving and how and when he or she died. This is always the hardest and most tearful meeting. For some, saying these things aloud makes them more real. Statements like "We were married for thirty-five years" or "My son was twenty-two years old" carry an end point. They reflect the reality that he will never be married for thirty-six years and her son will never be twenty-three. This shocking truth often catapults us back to the moment of death, the event that cannot be changed no matter how much we try to revisit it or wrest it from the clutches of the past. What the bereaved have taught me is that even in the most traumatic partings, one can find things for which to be grateful. And, as has been said time and again, gratitude is perhaps the surest toehold we have when scaling the cliff of grief.

One woman shared about losing her husband in a way that some would find incredibly traumatic. She, however, preferred to recognize the blessings inherent in the way they parted. She described to the group how she and her husband were coming home from a wonderful tropical vacation, one during which they had golfed, walked, and generally relaxed. As the plane was preparing for landing upon its return to New York, she turned to wake her sleeping husband, only to discover that he wasn't sleeping. He had died—without a sound or a signal. Perhaps he had sensed a head start on his ascent toward heaven from his vantage point there in the sky.

For some, this memory would be terribly distressing: the futile attempt to revive him, the removal of his body from the airplane, the trip to the hospital. She chose to see it differently. Not only was she grateful for the time they had together, but she was also thankful that he died so peacefully. They had just learned that he was in the very early stages of Alzheimer's disease and was facing a future of certain decline. Although more than willing to face this with him, she found comfort in knowing he was spared the difficult trajectory of this illness. How she thinks about their parting will continue to help her in her grieving.

When someone is dying from a terminal illness, there is more time to prepare emotionally, but this does not automatically ensure peace. An essential goal of hospice is helping the dying and their families to part well. This means keeping the one who is dying comfortable and assisting those involved in saying good-bye. It's also important to understand that not everyone *wants* to say good-bye. I have been approached many times by tearful family members asking me if they have to tell their loved ones, "It's okay to go." Perhaps they have heard this as a mandate, rather than a suggestion, from friends or medical professionals. Some may feel guilty for wanting to hold on to a loved one and worry that he or she, sensing this, may be suffering unnecessarily because of it. Others are afraid that giving "permission" might be frightening to the one who is dying. Whatever choice you made, if you were presented with that opportunity, was the right one. We do the best we can when faced with such heartbreaking circumstances, and you alone knew what might comfort or frighten the person you loved. When we are forced to part with someone, the only words that are universally correct are those spoken with love.

When my grandmother was nearing the end of her life at 106 years old, she was still very much herself mentally and only slightly failing physically. She was sleeping more and was less steady on her feet, although she refused to use a cane, saying, "It slows me down." She wondered why her birthdays seemed to keep coming, often noting that it was time for her to go and that she'd been here too long. One day my cousin, another granddaughter from out of town, came to visit her. Sitting quietly while our grandmother was napping, she thought she should encourage her to let go. And so she whispered, "It's okay, Grandma. You can go now. Grandpa is waiting for you and we will all be fine." At that, Grandma opened her eyes and said with a wry smile, "Relax. I'm not there yet." My cousin jumped and they both laughed. Several weeks later, when she *was* there, Grandma slipped away in her sleep without waiting for anyone's permission.

Not many people live so long and die so well. When death comes unexpectedly or without granting an opportunity to say good-bye, the bereaved can feel robbed of those final moments. Although I have been with hundreds of people as they were dying, I was not able to be with my own father in his last moments. His death came only hours after being rushed to the hospital. That morning, I received a call from my sister Laurie in Ohio. Based on a conversation with Mom, she didn't think Dad was doing well and so she was driving to their house, which was two hours away. After describing his symptoms, she asked me to call an ambulance; then I called my mom. Mom sounded concerned but not panicked. I asked her to tell me what was happening with Dad. When she did, I instinctively knew he was in kidney failure. I told her an ambulance was on the way and reassured her that Laurie would be there before it arrived. Meanwhile, I was stuck in New York due to a February nor'easter. Looking out my window, I felt desperately trapped by the swirling mountains of snow.

Though I wanted to brave the treacherous weather, the airports were closed and the roads were impassable. Mom, of course, understood. Because I never expected him to die that day, never expected not to make it there to say good-bye or to have one last moment, I hesitated when she wanted to put Dad on the phone. I assumed he was uncomfortable and possibly in distress, and I didn't want him to feel he had to speak with me. Now, looking back, I will always be grateful to my mom for ignoring my pleas not to bother him. She held the phone to his ear because he was too weak to hold it himself. Then I heard that familiar fatherly voice.

"Hey, Dad," I said. "What's going on?"

"Well, your boy isn't doing too well," he answered.

I tried to hear the message within the words. Was he frightened? Did he think this might be our last conversation? I couldn't be sure. His strength as a father was holding back the dam of any other emotions going on inside of him. In retrospect, I wonder if he was trying to spare me. I don't think he would have chosen to speak with me at that point, but he rallied when my mom pressed the phone to his cheek and told him I was on the line. Although my voice was shaking, I encouraged him to just relax and to go into that deep, meditative place of his. He was a mystic at heart and could connect to God more readily than anyone I knew. I told him I was snowed in but was getting a flight out in the morning. I told him that I loved him. "I love you too" were the last words he said to me. Even though we had said this to each other countless times and at the end of every conversation, I am grateful for that last expression of love. Without it, I would have to be okay. But remembering that last moment with him is comforting.

The pain of some partings is less easily remedied. A child who dies of an overdose, a parent who commits suicide, a friend who is a victim of violence—the post-traumatic shock of these circumstances magnifies our grief. When we do not leave each other well, when there is unfinished business, harsh words, or the trauma of an abrupt death, those who survive can suffer terribly. What do we do with the partings that are not "such sweet sorrow," to quote Shakespeare, but are truly agonizing?

One of the first things we need to do is to accept what has happened and what cannot be changed—the how and when of our loved ones' deaths. This is easier said than done. Where do we begin? The Serenity Prayer, attributed to Reinhold Niebuhr, may point us in the right direction. When we ask God to grant us the serenity to accept the things we cannot change, what we are asking for is a quieting of the heart, a stillness of the soul that might allow us to see more clearly the truth of our lives. It is here we surrender the illusion that we have control over everything that happens to us, that we can outfox misfortune and our own vulnerabilities and can escape this life unscathed. Serenity—the God-given kind—often resides in the broken places of our inmost beings. That's where we need it most; that's where we need God most. Praying for serenity helps clear a place inside of us where the noise of our pain and our bargaining and our wishful thinking gives way to humility and quiet acceptance.

Serenity may be difficult to achieve when one is grieving, but it is impossible without surrendering our hold on what we *wished* had happened. Fixating on the manner in which our loved ones have left us is sometimes a way to delay the full impact of their absence. When we keep coming back to the thing that haunts us, wondering what we could have done differently, we stay entrenched in what we cannot change. But when we have the courage to accept what has happened, we can at least open ourselves to the possibility of peace. If I were to keep returning to the snowy day that prevented me from seeing my dad one last time, or if I beat myself up for not visiting or calling more, I would essentially be binding him (or at least his memory) to a carousel of despair. But he is not there. He is not imprisoned in the things I wish I could change. His life is ongoing. The lives of those we love are ongoing. They were and are in God's hands. And they are safe there.

When sadness threatens to overwhelm us, we must ask ourselves if the love we shared was worth the pain we are now experiencing in loss. In other words, are you glad you knew this person, risked loving this person, or would you rather have been spared the suffering? Most of us would not trade a single moment with someone we love, even if it means that the parting one day will be devastating. In the words of Henri Nouwen,

> Every time we make the decision to love someone, we open ourselves to great suffering, because those we most love cause us not only great joy but also great pain. The greatest pain comes from leaving. When the child leaves home, when the husband or wife leaves for a long period of time or for good, when the beloved friend departs to another country or dies, the pain of the leaving can tear us apart.

> Still, if we want to avoid the suffering of leaving, we will never experience the joy of loving. And love is stronger than

fear, life stronger than death, hope stronger than despair. We have to trust that the risk of loving is always worth taking.*

Instead of dwelling on our partings, perhaps we should look with hope toward the joy of meeting again. We do not have to wait until our own deaths to do this. We can meet our loved ones in the things they loved and in the people they touched. We meet them in how we see the world and in the imprints they have left on us. I look forward to being reunited with those I love, and I have no doubt that I will be, but I try to live in the present moment, not in the past or in the future. Here and now, we have the opportunity to send love to those who have died, to thank them for their love, to pray for them, and to trust that their lives, and ours, are ongoing. There is sweetness in sorrow when we know we would do it all again, despite the pain. And there is comfort in the words that come after the final breath, those we cannot hear but feel nonetheless—the promise, *I'll see you soon.*

Meditation: Today I will not dwell on how my loved one parted from me. Instead, I will look forward to when we meet again.

Affirmation: By God's grace, I will see my loved one again in the place where there is neither sorrow nor separation.

---

* Henri J. M. Nouwen, *Bread for the Journey: A Daybook of Wisdom and Faith* (New York: HarperOne, 1997), 254.

Individually, we are one drop.
Together, we are an ocean.

—Ryunosuke Satoro

Quilt

Five months after the horrific shooting at Sandy Hook Elementary School in Newtown, Connecticut, a group of mothers came together on the shores of Rye, New York, a community fifty miles—and what must have seemed a lifetime—away. Organized by a few strong, caring women who wanted to do something to help, the day was offered as a gift to any mother from Newtown, whether she had lost a child or not. It was a way of saying that every mother's heart breaks when another loses a child, especially so unthinkably. And it recognized that these mothers, in particular, needed care.

It was a beautiful spring morning, just after Mother's Day, when two coach buses pulled up to deliver 109 moms from Newtown. Their numbers were matched by the women from Rye, each assigned to be a special guide and host to one from Newtown. The day was designed to offer a time apart for these women, a time of rest, reflection, and care. Activities included yoga and Pilates on the beach, nature walks, paddleboarding and kayaking, knitting, sewing, and bulb planting. There was a relaxation station set up for quiet reflection, with Gerbera daisies that could be tossed into the water. Massage therapists were at the ready with their tables and massage chairs lined up along the boardwalk. A lovely lunch was served, and a bench was dedicated to the families of Sandy Hook. But the most poignant moment for me was watching the mothers who chose to work on a quilt. The women from Rye had created its basic framework and had cut out twenty-six stars that could be stitched onto it by any mother who wanted to participate. Not all did. But the image of these women, many of whom had known terrible loss, sitting together, working together, remembering together, and creating something beautiful was powerful. Each stitch carried a prayer or a memory, each pull of the thread a tug on the heart. Maybe the focus needed to sew offered momentary relief from what the stars represented. It was not for me to ask. But these women were stitched together in their shared pain, and now we were loosely stitched there too. The quilt was an expression of loss and of hope, and it proclaimed, *We are Sandy Hook. We choose love.*

There is something comforting about the image of a quilt. It is often comprised of small pieces of cloth, scraps that are reminiscent of something else. The pieces are joined together in a pattern of one's choosing. One by one, they begin to form a story as they are sewn together and then arranged on the quilt. They may be attached by embroidery or by a simple stitch. Sometimes they are temporarily tacked on until the best arrangement is decided. It's almost impossible to rush the making of a quilt. If you try, the thread may break or the pattern may be lost. Quilts take time. Creating beauty and warmth from the remnants of things takes time.

When the pain of loss threatens to tear us apart, we need to find a way to stitch ourselves back together again. Most of us do not have the luxury of disintegrating, at least not completely for any length of time. We have family members to care for, jobs to do, or legal matters that require attention. Some have all of these on their plates. The most we are usually allowed, by others or ourselves, is some fraying at the edges. But the truth is, even when we appear to be holding it together, inside we can be in tatters.

What I learned from the Sandy Hook moms, among many, many things, is the importance of being open to support. The staggering pain of their individual losses was intimate, personal, and private—and yet they were willing to risk connection. The things they were able to share were mere fragments of the whole picture. They were remnants of the lives they had and the children they loved. For four hours of one spring day, they allowed us to be the backing of the quilt upon which their pieces could be arranged and shared, tacked and embroidered. We provided the framework; they brought the pieces. Just boarding the bus for Rye had been a leap of faith and an act of courage. It was also a stubborn affirmation of the goodness that still exists in a world torn by violence. In that moment, they refused to close themselves off or to succumb to despair. They chose to trust. They chose love.

These mothers are now a part of my quilt. Their stories have been embroidered next to mine. The pattern is still forming and changing, like a children's kaleidoscope that turns and turns. I do not always understand it. I cannot yet perceive its design, but it warms me when I am feeling frightened or alone. We are never alone in loss, not if we take a chance on each other. This does not mean giving advice; it just means showing up. Together we form a constellation, one that helps illuminate the night sky. God provides the backing to our starry quilt. If we stitch ourselves to the Divine and to one another, we can endure the heartbreak of loss. Our lights may then guide others on their journeys.

Meditation: Today I will gather the courage to share my tattered pieces with others who wish to help me with my grief.

Affirmation: My loved one and I are part of God's quilt, stitched together in a pattern of light.

> I have set my rainbow in the clouds, and it will be
> the sign of the covenant between me and the earth.
>
> —Genesis 9:13

Rainbows

"I asked my mom if she would give me a sign after she died to let me know she was okay," said the young woman, with a catch in her throat. "Since she always loved owls, I suggested maybe she could send me a message that way." Her beautiful green eyes filled with tears that hovered just on the edge of falling. They were an infinity pool of emotion. Her mother, to whom she had been very close, had recently died of ALS at the age of sixty. As she was nearing the end of her life, the woman worried about her daughter. She tried to reassure her that she would always be with her in spirit and that she was not afraid to die. While her daughter found comfort in this, she was still struggling. She did not possess her mother's unwavering faith or her unflinching certainty about the continuation of life after death. She *wanted* to believe it, but she was afraid to be disappointed. When I asked what her mother's response was to her request for an owl to serve as a spiritual messenger, she laughed.

"Well, Mom reminded me that we live in an urban area and that we hardly have a place for pigeons to land, much less an owl! But I said that's why I was asking for one. If I saw an owl, I would know for certain that it was from her."

"Sounds like a tall order," I said, smiling.

Many people ask their dying loved ones for a sign to reassure them that they are okay once they have gone. Even if they haven't asked, the bereaved often report seeing something that *feels* like a sign. Either way, the impulse comes from our deep yearning to have an ongoing connection to the deceased. It usually has less to do with a genuine concern about the condition or whereabouts of our loved ones' spirits after death, and more about the pain we anticipate feeling once they are gone. If someone is dying from an illness that affords time to think about and discuss such things, it is a way for those who love them to see beyond the finish line of death, to envision a future that somehow includes this person in some way. When death comes suddenly, those left behind may look for things that might be interpreted as signs.

Signs are a reassurance that we have not been abandoned or forgotten by those who have died. They serve as a bridge between this world and the one we can only imagine, the one where our loved ones have gone. Even people who are not religious sometimes report that they either have felt a presence or have been given what feels like a sign, and every sign that people describe is one that offers comfort. No one has ever told me they encountered a bad or ominous sign from a loved one.

Being open to signs also keeps us open to spiritual experiences and to the mystery of God. They can point the way to that which is greater than ourselves, the Holy Unknowable. By not slamming the door to this possibility, our hearts stay propped open despite sorrow's constant threat to lock them down. Openness keeps our hearts malleable and hopeful. It helps us feel that the wall that separates this world and the next is permeable, if it exists at all. Encountering what we believe to be a sign ignites a little spark in our spirits. It warms us with a feeling of presence and closeness to our loved ones. Basking in this warmth, we feel grateful and loved. And these feelings of gratitude for being seen and remembered by those who have died is also a way to feel seen and remembered by God. If our loved ones are close by, and they are close to God, then we, in turn, are closer too. If they are in God's hands, then perhaps we, too, are held.

In some ways it doesn't matter if the signs we experience are actually sent from the Beyond or are a way for us to remember and to feel remembered. One woman I know feels especially close to her mother when she encounters hearts in unexpected places: a seashell, a puddle, a cloud. Each time she sees one, it's like her mom is blowing her a little kiss: *Yes, dear, I'm here. I see you and I'm with you.* Others have told me of sensing their loved ones in a particular bird that comes to sit on their windowsill or in butterflies that appear at odd times and in strange ways.

My son Alex had one such experience. It was his freshman year in college and he had just completed a football game—the first game he had ever played with no family member there to watch or to cheer for him, to support or to worry for him. He had chosen to go to school in Ohio, even though it was a long way from New York, in part to be close to my father. He knew his grandfather, Poppie, would be at every game, even if his dad and I could not always be there. But Poppie died six months before the first game of the season. As Alex began making the long walk off the field, he was feeling rather alone. He looked up at the beautiful blue sky. *Wish you could have been here, Poppie,* he thought. Then, looking down, he noticed a beautiful butterfly sitting lightly on his right shoulder pad. It opened and closed its wings, as if waving hello. As he continued to walk, he had the profound sense of his grandfather's presence. For over a hundred yards, with other players bumping into him and people loudly making their way out of the stands, the butterfly never left his shoulder. When he reached the entrance to the locker room, he gently encouraged it to fly away. For Alex (and for me) it was a sign of Poppie's presence and ongoing support.

I had a similar experience at the funeral of a young fireman. Only thirty-six years old when he died of a rare cancer, the man was beloved by the department and the community. As the chaplain to the fire department, I took my place with the other uniformed personnel to line the driveway leading up to the church. As we stood there silently, a large blue-and-black butterfly came to rest directly on my chaplain's badge. I couldn't remember the last time I had seen this particular type of butterfly. Orange and black—yes. Blue and black—hardly ever. I nudged the chief, who was standing next to me. His eyes went wide. I expected the butterfly to take off, especially when the fire trucks drove by, leading the way for the hearse, but it did not. It kept its place on my badge until the fireman's casket was taken inside the church. Then it flew away.

I believe in the possibility of signs. God sent one, after all, as a reminder of a promise. Each time we see a rainbow, we are to remember not only God's promise to the earth but also our responsibility to live as God's people. On a recent anniversary of September 11, I was driving into New York City when a giant rainbow appeared in the sky. In the next moment, an airplane rose from LaGuardia, its image momentarily shellacked onto the rainbow. That's when I started to cry. I wanted to think it was God's way of saying, *Never again will I allow such a thing to happen,* but I knew that was not the case. When I let go of such wishful thinking, I felt God saying, *I'm here.* And that promise is unwavering. It doesn't depend on life going well. God is with us, despite what we do to each other and to the earth, and despite the pain we feel. I do not need signs to believe in God or to trust that those who have died are alive and well in some other form, but they bolster me when I am feeling down. Similarly, my children do not need me to tell them I love them as often as I do, because they know this to be true. But I tell them anyway, over and over again, so that it might be like a never-ending fountain within them. I'm not sure what sign I will try to give them when I die, but I hope they will see me in each other and in the awareness of God's presence in their lives.

As for the daughter who asked her mother for an owl, this is what she later told me:

A few weeks after Mom died, I was driving down the park-way—or, trying to drive. It was rush hour and the traffic was terrible. Of course, I was thinking of Mom and missing her terribly. "Oh, Mom," I remember whispering, "where are you?

How are you?" Inching along, I looked up. And what did I see? Yup, you guessed it: an owl. An owl! Sitting right there in broad daylight on a telephone wire. "Mom!" I gasped. Then the traffic started to move and I watched it for as long as I could in my rearview mirror. If anyone could pull this off, it would be her. She's the strongest person I've ever known.

Sometimes signs come in unexpected ways; sometimes they don't seem to come at all. But it doesn't mean we shouldn't watch for them. What we are really watching for is the reassurance that life goes on, that we are loved and connected, and that one day we will see our loved ones again. If it feels like you've been given a sign, write it down because you might forget it one day. You might doubt its veracity and power. So many people have shared their signs with me, and I have received so many myself, that I can hardly remember them anymore. And if you do not believe in signs, create your own. Commit yourself to giving special thanks for your loved one every time you see a cardinal, for example, or each time you help someone in need. How we live is the most vivid sign of our loved ones' ongoing lives and their legacies. Be a sign of love and let God do the rest.

Meditation: Today I will meditate on the special ways my loved one comes to me and on the love that continues to flow.

Affirmation: By opening my heart, I open my eyes to the presence of the Divine and the signs that I am given.

Remember not only to say the right thing in the right place, but far more difficult still, to leave unsaid the wrong thing at the tempting moment.

—Benjamin Franklin

Sayings

If I had kept a book of all the insensitive things that have been said to those who are grieving, it would be woefully substantial. The nicest, most well-meaning people manage to say the most hurtful things. Whether out of nervousness or a desire to quickly "fix" someone's sorrow, the temptation is to offer a platitude and move on. The problem is, what is left in the wake of an empty phrase is often a fresh wound to the grieving person's heart. Whether these comments come from a friend or a relative, a coworker or a neighbor, whether spoken at church, at temple, at the funeral, or months later over coffee, the impact is the same. An insensitive remark can act as a stop sign for the bereaved. It says, in essence, "I don't want to hear about your pain; I want you to be better" or "I don't know what else to say." Platitudes do not invite conversation. They silence the one who is hurting and can effectively plug up the ocean of feelings that may need to be expressed.

An insensitive remark rarely makes the bereaved feel better—it only relieves the discomfort of the person saying it.

Most of us have been on the receiving end of an inadvertently hurtful remark. When one is grieving, it cuts more deeply. What is particularly painful or triggering for one person may not have the same negative effect on someone else, but one can never be sure. This is one reason people find such relief and comfort in being part of a bereavement group. It just might be the one place where platitudes are not offered, advice is not given, and *should*s are never allowed. No one ever says, for example, "Try to be strong" or "You should just keep busy" or, my hot button, "Everything happens for a reason." Instead, you hear things like "What helps me is . . ." and "I'm struggling with . . ." and "Grieve as long as you need to." People are there to share their stories and to listen to the stories of others. They know there is no express lane when it comes to grief and no one-size-fits-all remedy. Comfort is found not in what people say to each other but in how they listen to one another. That is the miracle. That is also the lesson. Unless one is truly willing to be with other people in their pain, to listen with love and empathy without trying to fix them, the mouth is better off closed.

You who are grieving already know these things. You have your own hot buttons, the things people have said that hurt, silenced, or bothered you. You have a better sense than most about what *not* to say to someone who has just lost a loved one, but your head and your spirit might still be spinning from something that was said to you. Perhaps looking at a few of these will help the wound begin to mend.

"Everything happens for a reason." As stated earlier, this is a phrase that some may find helpful but many do not, especially when it is said after a death. Personally, I find no comfort in this blanket statement. When someone says this to me, or to someone else who is grieving, what I hear is a complete invalidation of the need to grieve. If everything happens for a reason, the inference is that the reason is divinely ordained and we should accept it, even if we do not understand it. All I need to refute this is to think about the Holocaust, terrorist attacks, and the deaths of children. If there is a reason for these, I'm not so sure I want to know.

"It must have been God's will." This phrase is a close cousin to the first. Again, it renders the grief-stricken silent. How can one argue with that? Reverend William Sloane Coffin, renowned pastor and writer, suggested that religious people often say these words "for self-protection, to pretty up a situation whose bleakness they simply couldn't face." Reverend Coffin intimately knew the pain of grief. He lost his twenty-three-year-old son in a car accident one dark and stormy night, when the car he was driving went off the road and into Boston Harbor. In response to those who suggested God had a reason for his son's death or that it was God's will, Coffin wrote,

> The one thing that should never be said when someone dies is, "It is the will of God." Never do we know enough to say that. My own consolation lies in knowing that it was *not* the will of God that Alex die; that when the waves closed over the

sinking car, God's heart was the first of all our hearts to break.*

I believe these things to be true for all of our loved ones—that we never know enough to say something is God's will and that God's heart is the first of all of ours to break. When our hearts are broken, they cannot hold words or theology. These stream through the cracks and leave us empty. What they need is the healing balm of patience and friendship, of empathy and support. Instead of sending the bereaved off on a scavenger hunt in search of reasons, true friends are able to sit with them in the senselessness of it all and in the sorrow. And God? "God," wrote Coffin, "doesn't go around this world with his finger on triggers, his fist around knives, his hands on steering wheels."† Instead, God gives us the strength to get through whatever happens.

"Time heals all wounds." Don't you wish you had a nickel for every time this has been said to you? Ironically, it's usually said at a time when time has no meaning. In the clutches of grief, minutes can feel like hours and days can pass in a blur. How can time heal anything, especially the wound of losing someone, when one is in free fall, catapulted outside the normal structure of our days? Some suggest it is not time that heals but what we do with the time. While there may be some truth in this, it also implies that grief is a wound that *can*

---

* William Sloane Coffin, *The Collected Sermons of William Sloane Coffin,* vol. 2, *The Riverside Years* (Louisville, KY: Westminster John Knox Press, 2008), 4.

† Coffin, *Collected Sermons,* 3–4.

be healed. Rose Kennedy, wife of Joseph Kennedy Sr., put it this way: "It has been said that time heals all wounds. I don't agree. The wounds remain. Time—the mind, protecting its sanity—covers them with some scar tissue and the pain lessens, but it is never gone."* This is, perhaps, the bravest thing spoken about time and grief. It not only rings true but also alleviates the pressure that grieving people often feel to heal and to "get over it." After all, how much time is enough? What's the timetable for grief? And if the wound is *not* healed in, say, a year, does that mean they have somehow failed in their grieving?

When a person says this phrase to someone in pain, it doesn't feel empathetic or helpful; it feels like a dismissal. Perhaps a better thing to say, if we have to say anything at all about time, is, "Take your time. Take all the time you need. You are learning to live without an essential part of yourself." Death doesn't feel like a wound; it feels more like an amputation. We cannot grow back the part of ourselves that we have lost. We cannot simply stitch together the hole left by our loved ones' absence. We need to learn how to walk again. This takes time, yes, but time will not fix it. What it may do is allow scar tissue to form so that walking is not so painful.

"I know how you feel." This well-meaning expression of empathy can sometimes be like a U-turn in a conversation about our grief. Instead of encouraging the bereaved to share their feelings, people who say this, intentionally or not, have just shifted the focus to themselves. "Okay, you've just made this about you" is what I would like to say in response. The statement "I know how you feel" practically begs

---

* Rose Fitzgerald Kennedy, *Times to Remember* (New York: Doubleday, 1974), 304.

the bereaved to ask the person speaking whom it is that he or she has lost. For what the person is really saying is "I know how you feel, so ask me how I know. I'm in pain too. Ask me what happened." This is the message that is silently broadcast, and it's usually not helpful. It doesn't give the bereaved a chance to fully express how he or she is feeling since the listener already claims to know. We can hardly imagine how another person feels on a good day, much less a day of deep sorrow. What's more, can we really hear what another person is saying if we are eagerly poised to share about our own losses? Perhaps it would be more helpful to offer the words "I'm here for you" or "I can share some things that have helped me, if you ever want to talk."

On a related note, the words "I can't imagine how you must be feeling" carry the subliminal message "and I don't want to." It's like telling someone that what he is going through is so horrific you don't even want to sit with him in your imagination. This doesn't feel like empathy; it feels like a recoiling. And it can be painfully isolating for the one who is grieving. If this has been said to you in your time of grief, how did you respond? How *do* you respond? One option is to say, "Well, it's not something anyone wants to imagine, but here I am." Or, "I'm not asking you to imagine it. I'm just asking you to be here for me." Unfortunately, the bereaved are usually forced to be the teachers when it comes to grief. The other option is just to shake the person's hand and move on. You actually don't have to say anything at all.

The catchphrases could go on and on: "He's in a better place." "At least she's not suffering." "Cherish the memories." None of these are very inviting or comforting. In my mind, I've just been told that (a) you know where my loved one's soul is, as well as how I think about it; (b) I'm selfish for being sad, since my loved one was suffering; and (c) I should hold on to my memories because there won't be any more new ones made and they may slip away from me. People say these things not to hurt us but because they do not know what else to say. Grief is scary. What cannot be fixed is scary. When grieving people share with each other the various things that have been said to them, they tend to laugh, and laughter helps them let it all go. They trust they are among people who *do* understand and *are* willing to imagine and *can* listen without trying to tidy up the messiness of loss.

Finally, what seems to be growing in popularity, and diminishing in meaning, is the phrase "My thoughts and prayers are with you." Thoughts and prayers can be two wings of a dove. They move harmoniously together. When they take flight, they can lift the spirits of the broken and cross the expanse between two people who care about each other. Unfortunately, this has become as reflexive as saying "God bless you" after someone sneezes. If someone says this to me, or writes it on my Facebook wall, I want to answer, "Yes, please do pray for me." Who knows—maybe they will. If, in turn, I write, "You're in my prayers," I make a concerted effort to remove my fingers from the keyboard, bow my head, and actually say a prayer.

While trying to express sympathy, whether awkwardly or with a cliché, most people are doing their best. What they want to say is "I'm sorry you're hurting." Maybe they shrink from the sucker punch that death packs because they have been hit themselves a time or two. So perhaps we should just be gentle with each other. We should forgive each other for the clumsy expressions that trounce on the toes of our hearts. After all, we are in this dance together but none of us know the steps. We are reaching for straws when what we desperately want is a golden cord or some magic beans to scale our way into heaven for one last hug, one last conversation. When we search for words instead of searching for each other, we will always fall short. So much more can be said with a listening ear.

Meditation: Today I will let go of the hurtful things said to me since my loved one's death. I will listen for the words I need to hear and will trust that others are trying their best.

Affirmation: I will be gracious and understanding in the face of clumsy condolences.

Treasure

Mom was cleaning out what used to be my brother's closet but, in recent years, had functioned mostly for storage. Joey had moved out long ago, first for college and then to pursue a career halfway across the country. Thumbing through the clothes, she began removing those bound for donation, a journey long overdue. Most were odds and ends, well-worn shirts passed down from brother to brother, old baseball uniforms, pants that no longer fit, a wool jacket. Occasionally she would pause when something triggered a memory—that shirt he wore for his high school picture, the sweatshirt with his fraternity letters—and she would run her hand lightly over the material, like a benediction, before gently placing it on the growing pile. When yet another castoff had been removed, what she saw next prompted a soft gasp. It was a faded striped T-shirt, a child's, one that had been snuggled there amidst other memories for over forty years. The child it had belonged to never outgrew it, never needed another size or hand-me-down. He had been Joey's best friend, her best friend's son, and he had died when he was six years old.

Joey and Matthew had been inseparable. They were as close to brothers as nonbrothers could be. In some ways they were closer—they were spirit brothers. Hours before Mattie died, the families had been picnicking together. When he started screaming about having a headache, the picnic was quickly packed away. Everyone piled into one big station wagon and headed home. No one could ever have imagined that Mattie would be gone from a brain aneurism before the sun would rise the next morning.

Only the immediate family was allowed to view his body before burial. We were later told he was dressed in the Native American "Indian suit" that he had loved so much. Not even my mother was permitted to see him, although it was she who had washed and ironed that suit for his burial. The only exception was Joey. Matthew's parents were concerned that Joey might not be able to accept the reality of his friend's death because he was only five years old at the time. I've never asked him about this—about what he remembers or how he felt—but I know it left an indelible mark on who he is.

The shirt in the closet was the one Mattie wore in his first-grade picture. His mother gave it to Joey, perhaps as a touchstone or a talisman, something to remember him by. It was given out of love and concern for him. He wore it constantly. And when he outgrew it, he tucked it away and had obviously kept it all these years, pristine and silent, like a pair of angel wings waiting patiently for its angel to retrieve them. When she found the shirt hanging there, Mom called Joey to ask what he wanted her to do with it. "Keep it," he said quietly.

"Please just hold on to it for me." She was now the guardian of buried treasure.

Jesus said, "Where your treasure is, there your heart will be also."* Mattie's shirt was a treasure, not because it was made with gold thread, but rather because it was a portal to the place in his heart where Joey keeps Matthew. Something of Matthew—and of Joey—still lives in that shirt because his friend wore it. It proves that he was real and he is remembered and that true friendship doesn't end with death. True love doesn't end with death.

It's usually not the expensive gifts or belongings that we treasure most when someone dies. It's the simple everyday ones—a cup, a library card, a rolling pin, a favorite sweater. These provide a tactile connection to the one who has died. Sometimes they are valued for the memories they trigger, sometimes for the remnants of energy, personality, and even DNA that they carry. Each is a key that fits a sacred place in our hearts, a place where we shore up our reserves of every loving word exchanged, every lesson we have learned, and all that we hold dear about the person we are missing. Sometimes we learn the full value of things only after they are gone. That's why when someone we love dies, we often feel robbed of an irreplaceable treasure.

At the age of eleven, a young girl I know lost her mother quite suddenly. Since then, Sorcha has become very special to me and has taught me volumes about grief and the difficulty of living with unfathomable loss. In fact, *treasure* was her word, not mine, setting the theme for this chapter. As we talked about this, she wrote me the following note:

---

* Matthew 6:21.

If I were you, I would write about treasure! Like when I go rooting through all my mom's old stuff, like her clothes or old handwritten papers. It's comforting for me to find and it's treasure to me. And it makes me cry. That's what I have to treasure now of her . . .

It's like she left keepsakes for me to continuously find to be reminded she is here.

These also let me figure her out more. I have recently found that in every wallet, handbag, jacket—you name it—my mom carried tape measures with her at all times. Life of an architect—but the life of my mom too.

Sorcha is obviously wise beyond her seventeen years. She has reminded me that it is possible to find flecks of treasure long after someone dies. We do not have to hoard or to hold on to everything we find—not at all. *Things* will not bring our loved ones back. We can, however, be aware of the small gifts they have left behind, like stones that still carry the warmth of the sun. My father's old Cincinnati Bengals sweatshirt is like that for me. I wear it when I write, and I feel his guiding hand. The essence of his love and creativity is still palpable in the thread, even though I have washed it many times now.

Maybe the things we treasure emanate some sort of homing signal. Perhaps they serve as spiritual beacons in the night, flashing a message between this world and the next: *You are not forgotten! I love you! I feel you!* Even if we have nothing tangible to touch or to hold, we can manifest treasures in our minds and access them in our hearts. This is slightly different from revisiting or cherishing our memories. Memories are precious, but they are part of the past. The things we treasure, whether a facet of a memory, a particular aspect of a loved one, or a tangible talisman, we carry with us—always. They continue to inform us about our loved ones and remind us that life is ongoing, that we can still learn from those who have died and can still feel their presence. The smell of Old Spice will forever be my grandfather. My bony wrists and the veins in my hands are remnants of my grandmother. These small things are treasures that will never lose their value and cannot be taken from me.

Each thing that we treasure bears a certain aspect of our loved ones. To hold these things or to think of them with intentionality is to open our hearts to the gift of who they were and are, and the love that we shared. Our treasures should not fill us with sadness; they should inspire deep gratitude for having known these special people. They are keepsakes that lead us to the mystery of our loved ones and the relationships we still have with them. If we are willing to stay with the mystery and the wonder inherent in the treasures they have left us, instead of being pulled into the past where they no longer live, our understanding of them will continue to unfold and we will feel them near. Memories make me sad at times, but the things I treasure always fill me with joy.

Meditation: Today I will hold, in my hand or in my heart, something I treasure from my loved one. I will open my heart to the love that continues to flow and to the mystery waiting to be discovered.

Affirmation: My loved one has not left me empty handed. My heart is full of treasure.

> Ever has it been that love knows not its
> own depth until the hour of separation.
>
> —Kahlil Gibran

Until

One of my favorite songs by George and Ira Gershwin is "I Was Doing Alright." Made famous by Ella Fitzgerald, it is essentially a song about feeling happy and content with your life until the moment you meet the person with whom you fall in love. Once that happens, life is never the same. You can't go back—nor would you want to.

Things that never bothered you before—the rain, being alone—are newly imbued with the awareness of absence when you love someone and then are separated from him or her. If you've never enjoyed the sweetness of a strawberry, you don't crave it. If you've always lived alone, you don't miss a warm body next to you. If you've never given your heart to someone, chances are it's never been broken—but it's also never burst with joy. "I was doing alright till you came by!" wrote Ira, with a sly wink. It's an acknowledgment that we can be happy on our own, but this happiness does not compare to the kind we feel after we have experienced love, whether for a beloved, a newborn, or a friend.

Until is a word that often tethers us to a point in the past. It encompasses everything that happened leading up to a particular event. Then a line is drawn in the sand, separating a before and an after: *This was my life until* that *happened.* Our lives are full of befores and afters. Some events on the *after* side of the equation are incredibly happy: *I didn't know what deep joy was until I had my daughter. I felt so alone until I met my best friend. I was floundering until I realized my calling.* These kinds of musings propel us forward and inspire gratitude. In them, we recognize the blessings that have changed our lives for the better. For someone who is grieving, however, the blessings feel (at least for a time) as if they are on the other side of the equation. Because of this, the bereaved sometimes find themselves combing through the events that preceded a death, looking for clues that could somehow change the outcome. *She was doing pretty well until she broke her hip. He was okay until he had that reaction to the medication. They seemed fine until they stopped for that last drink. My life was happy until Mom died.*

When it comes to the death of a loved one, *until* separates the life we knew and loved from the one we are now living. What's more, it's a life we did not choose but rather one that has happened to us. Part of what leaves us bewildered is precisely that lack of choice. We may have chosen to get married, for example, but we did not choose the moment of separation imposed by the death of our spouse. We may have chosen to have a baby, but we certainly did not choose for that child to predecease us. The feeling of powerlessness in the face of death can often send us flying into despair, especially if we keep returning to the moment when *before* became *after:* "I was doing alright till . . ." Unlike the sentiment expressed in the song, what follows a death is not an increase in happiness but the loss of it. The wistfulness inherent in this way of thinking keeps us on that pivotal point of the seesaw. The best parts of the past are lost when we are not able to carry the joy of them into the present moment, much less into the future. Holding on to the past is different from being grateful for it. If we view our present lives as but the charred remains of what was, something dies inside of us. And what was given to us by our loved ones, what we learned from them, and what we are able to carry with us in the embers are left to grow cold. We alone are able to keep the flames that were ignited by our relationships burning. To do this, we need to guard the sparks that remain and breathe new life into them by being open to the ongoing possibility of connection and happiness.

Those we love will always be a part of us. Will we miss them? Of course we will! It is terribly painful to begin the journey of living without them. But refusing to take even one wobbly step toward a new way of experiencing all they have left us does not honor them and will not bring them close again. It may take time, maybe years, for us to take that first step out of the darkness of despair and the shadows of the past into the dawn of a new present. But when we do, we will not be disappointed. Our loved ones are waiting for us there, not just in the future when we join them in what is to come, but in the present, where their loving energy can still be felt.

There are times, many times, that I think of my dad and yearn to hear his voice or absorb the warmth of his physical presence. All of the ways I knew him before he died are there in those memories. But I also know that I am experiencing his love and presence in new ways. He is no longer constrained to the limitations of human life, or even personality. He is now fully the spirit that, for a time, inhabited the familiar frame I knew as my dad. My relationship with him is ongoing. It continues to grow, and he continues to teach me. When I listen for his guidance, I can hear his voice in my heart. When I am lonely for him, I feel his presence. I know this is different for me than it is for my mother. Her day-to-days were built around their life together and the intimacy they shared. But I believe that she, too, can draw strength from the well of that relationship, a well that will never run dry.

We are individual souls who find ourselves living a human life in community. This earth is our schoolhouse, designed for us to learn and grow—and, in order to do that, we need each other. The love we have for another person always points to a bigger love, the Source of love. Perhaps we feel at home with those we love because this feeling reminds us of the soul's original home. We feel less lonely for God when we love someone, for we were *with* God until we were here, until we were born. The earth would feel like a foreign land if not for the way God has saturated it with love.

We can feel at home here by loving what God has created, by caring for the planet, by showing compassion to God's creatures, and by recognizing love's incarnation in each other. We are all little sparks of the Divine. When we love another person, we not only increase our own sparks but we also create a warm and dancing flame that is more than the sum of its parts. When our loved ones are gone, it feels for a time as if they have taken all warmth with them. We yearn for them, specifically and individually. The fire within us may even feel as if it has gone out for a time. But it has not. The sparks of love cannot be extinguished by death because love is not constrained to this world. The hand that lit the match will not leave us shivering in the cold. Our task is to be good stewards of the spark we have been given and the flame that has been created by knowing and loving another person. The flame of love can never dwindle unless we insist on confining it to the past.

Maybe the only *until* that has the possibility of comfort is "until we meet again." It encompasses the entirety of our relationships with those who have died. It honors the past, acknowledging all that has been. It accepts the present, including the responsibility we have to continue on the journey, despite the pain. And it looks with love toward the certainty of reunion. As for me, I choose to meet my dad in everything that reminds me of him. I meet him when my dogs make me smile, because it reminds me of his love of animals. I meet him in the moments I show compassion to a stranger, because that is how he lived. I meet him in the words that sometimes appear almost by themselves at my fingertips, because my writing is from him.

Perhaps this is a glimpse of what Jesus was trying to teach us when he said, after his death, that we can continue to meet him in the hungry, the thirsty, the stranger, the sick, the naked, the imprisoned, and all those who need our care. We will feel the nearness of his presence when we see him in each other. "Truly I tell you, whatever you did for one of the least of these brothers and sisters of mine, you did for me," he said.* Until we meet our loved ones again, in spirit form,

---

* Matthew 25:40.

we can meet them here and now in everything they have taught us, in the love they gave us, and in our willingness to share that love with others. We cannot replace each other's losses, but we can tenderly hold the sacred space, giving love the oxygen it needs to keep burning. "Until we meet again" is not passive; it is a promise that requires action. If we are to recognize our loved ones in the world to come, we must begin by honoring the remnants they have left and kindling them into ongoing expressions of love.

Until you meet your loved one again, face to face, meet him every day in what and whom he loved; meet her every day in acts of kindness that draw you closer to her and, therefore, to God. *Until* is only as long as one makes it. It is no longer than the time it takes to strike a match, to see beauty, and to open your heart.

Meditation: Today I will not linger on my loved one's death. Instead, I will contemplate the good I can do until we meet again.

Affirmation: God's grace accompanies me through all my befores and afters, from one moment until the next.

You never know how strong you are
until being strong is your only choice.

—Bob Marley

Violence

In this world of ours, it is nearly impossible to speak of death without acknowledging that some have lost their lives in unspeakable ways. How I wish it were not so. Coping with the loss of a loved one is hard, even when we have had time to say good-bye and to emotionally prepare. When death comes suddenly, the shock of it can feel like a cannonball to the heart. When it is sudden *and* violent, it can tear us to pieces. The horror we feel, combined with the loss itself, can send us into a pit of despair from which it feels there is no returning. Violent deaths can be the result of crime, terrorism, mass shootings, war, and injuries that may be self-inflicted. Trusting that the ones who died are free from whatever horror precipitated their deaths offers some consolation—but what of the bereaved who must live with this reality?

A very dear friend of mine had a teenaged sister who was murdered almost forty years ago. The case shook the entire state in which they lived. But it was more than just a case to the family; it was Carlotta, their precious, irreplaceable girl. Most people were kind, some were curious or voyeuristic, and some stayed away simply because they didn't know what to say. The fact that the murderers were apprehended, confessing details that could never be unheard or forgotten, offered a measure of relief but not consolation. True consolation isn't a matter of justice being served, although that certainly is important. Justice reestablishes order and creates a safer place not only to live but also to grieve. I'm not sure what my friend Sherrerd felt when her sister's killers were finally executed years later, but I don't think it was consolation. Numb relief might be a closer description. She will always live with the pain of missing her sister and the terrible knowledge of how Carlotta was taken from her. What was also taken from her was the chance to be part of a family that was not torn by violence. At nineteen, Sherrerd was expected to return to college immediately after the funeral to finish her classes. What's more, she was supposed to do so without the support that such a devastating trauma requires. Her sister's murder not only took the life of a beautiful young girl, but it also changed the very fabric of her family's life and the future that would unfold for all of them.

An extraordinary twenty-year-old college student was living in Egypt in the summer of 2013. Although he was aware of the unrest in Egypt during that time, his idealism and values inspired him to commit his summer to teaching English to Egyptian children and to improving his Arabic. By all accounts, he was thriving with the children and was beloved by his host family. One day a street protest broke out in Alexandria. For reasons we will never know, Andrew was stabbed in the chest and died from his injuries. What should have been a few months spent away from his family and friends turned out to be a lifetime. No one could have imagined it. His tragic death sent a hurricane of shock, horror, and profound grief through his family and his wide circle of friends. My daughter was one of those friends. She said that he was a wonderful person, one who had that intangible, special *something* about him, that he was full of hope and kindness and was universally loved. Aside from being devastated by the loss of her friend, she was haunted by the violent way in which he died and by picturing him so far away from his family when it happened.

When the towers of the World Trade Center came down, mass killing hit home. As a chaplain to the morgue at Ground Zero, it was difficult for me to bless the bodies of those who had died. But it is a different kind of difficult to look into the eyes of the children who lost parents or relatives that day. Some of them are now my children's friends, encountered in college and bonded for life. Whether they want to or not, they carry the imprint of September 11 on their hearts and spirits. They belong to the growing community of those who have lost loved ones due to terrorism in places like Oklahoma, Connecticut, California, Florida, France, Belgium, Israel, Palestine, Iraq, Nigeria, Germany, and, sadly, too many other places to name. Sometimes it seems the world has gone mad with killing. Whether there is more violence in the world today than in the past or just more awareness of it due to our access to information, who can say?

Unlike the slow unwinding of a life that has reached old age or

the end of a terminal illness, a life cut short by violence leaves those
who remain tattered and in shock. The post-traumatic stress that follows is distinct from other losses. It can bombard the bereaved with
anxiety and a feeling of vulnerability. Sleep may become elusive because dreams turn into nightmares that are filled with haunting images. After a loved one has died violently, it is hard to feel safe and very
easy to feel angry. If the death is of a communal or public nature and
the media gets involved, one can suddenly be thrust into the public
eye, which carries its own stressors. For those who do not wish to
publically state the cause of death, the need for privacy can be interpreted as a door that is closed to support of any kind. This can feel
very isolating. Shame, anger, fear, or a feeling of helplessness may set
in. And it may take years before one is ready or able to begin the journey of unpacking all those emotions. Until then, the bereaved can feel
as if they are walking around in a suit of heavy armor. It may protect
them from the insensitive comments of others or from the full extent
of their pain, but it also weighs them down, slowing their ability to
heal.

Grief that follows a violent death is in a category all its own, with
many subdivisions. Families of police officers killed in the line of duty,
for example, or families of those they have been entrusted to serve and
protect can feel a grim sense of community with others who have
known a similar loss. Likewise, parents who have lost sons or daughters to war or to a drunk driver, to an overdose or to gun violence may
feel less isolated in their grief when in the company of other grieving
parents. In the midst of the unfathomable, we search for those who

might be able to share an ounce of our pain. It's not that misery loves company but, rather, that misery yearns for solace and for compassion, and this is often found in the eyes of those who *know.*

Anyone who has lost a loved one to suicide also needs special understanding when it comes to grief. Sometimes shame and guilt wrap themselves around those who were closest to the person who died, making it difficult to share and process their feelings. Fear of judgment keeps family members quiet; anger at the one who died makes them feel guilty. The peace that sometimes accompanies those who have cared for a terminally ill loved one is completely unobtainable, as is the desire to share the details of a loved one's last tender moments. With suicide, those last moments are anything but tender. After her boyfriend ended his life by putting a gun to his head, a girl shared how she was faced with the task of helping his family clean up. The police had come and gone, the body had been removed, and the boy's family could not face the room where he had died. She and a friend did for them what they could not do for themselves—scrub the walls of his blood. The walls came clean, but their minds could not be cleansed of the traumatic way in which he chose to end his life. The memories of this would remain.

If you have lost a loved one to suicide, know this: the one you loved was in pain. You may not have seen it. You may never be able to understand it. It is not your fault. You could not have prevented it. It is a terrible thing to have happened, and it leaves so much hurt and confusion for those who are left behind. I hope you might find comfort in knowing that your loved one is no longer in the kind of pain that prompted this decision. He is restored. She is joyful. He is probably sorry for the pain he is causing you. Most of us do the best we can in life with the raw materials and the situations we've been dealt. Some people lose the thread. They lose faith that life is worth living. If you feel helpless in the face of suicide, remember, there is always one thing you can do: you can send love to your loved one. Pray for her to know healing and peace. Forgive him. By praying for your loved one, your spirit will also begin to mend. This does not mean you will be suddenly free of pain, but you will not be paralyzed by it, at least not forever.

After surviving the violent death of a loved one, it is important to remember that you *have* survived, you are alive. For now, that may be the best you can hope for: to simply stay alive, to keep your heart beating and your shoes on the right feet. Your loved one would not want it any other way. If you withered away or chose not to live, part of them would also wither. Your loved one's life was taken once. Most likely, he or she had no choice in the matter—but you do. How tragic it would be for what is left of them to vanish with you in the abandoning of your own life. By living, you carry a part of who they are with you. If you crumble and surrender to sorrow, something of them will be lost. And so you should live, not just for yourself, but for your loved one as well.

When death comes with shocking brutality, it leaves in its wake a debris field of sorrow and a sense of violation. This is a time to surround yourself with people you trust and love. You have no obligation to answer the questions of the curious or even the well-meaning. In fact, you don't have to say anything at all. "I'm doing the best I can" will have to suffice. Violence may have taken your loved one's life, but it doesn't have to take over your memories of the person she was and is to you. We can reclaim the images we have of our loved ones by wresting them from those terrible final moments. We do not have to surrender more than what has already been stolen from us. A man with a gun can take the life of one we love, but he can never take her spirit, can never take his personality and soul. And so it is our task to reclaim these precious parts, gathering them one by one and refashioning them with the shattered pieces of our own hearts.

Our loved ones, however they might have died, are not constrained to their last moments on earth. They simply aren't. So we should not keep them there either. Although they are no longer suffering, we sometimes inadvertently keep them on the front lines of pain by continuously reliving or imagining their final moments. To free your loved one, try talking to him in your heart. Tell her that you feel broken, that you are sorry she suffered so, that you miss and love her. Trusting that they are completely restored—and happy beyond imagining—allows us to release them from the pain of their final moments. In doing so, we release ourselves as well. As we reach for our loved ones' hands, we trust that their hands are holding God's and God is holding ours. Together we form a circuit of love. God never lets go. Violence will never have the last word. The darkness of despair cannot extinguish the light of God's unwavering love for us. When we are most in pain, we must hold fast to this promise: "The light shines in the darkness, and the darkness has not overcome it."[*]

---

[*] John 1:5.

Meditation: Today I will not dwell on how my loved one died. Instead, I will remember an aspect of him or her for which I am especially grateful.

Affirmation: The world cannot destroy what it never created: the eternal life and spirit of my loved one.

> What I feared has come upon me;
>> what I dreaded has happened to me. . . .
> Why have you made me your target?
>
> —Job 3:25; 7:20

Why

It's staggering how one small word can convey the weight of human anguish. Whether we are diagnosed with an illness, flattened by a catastrophe, or standing by the coffin of someone we love, the question of why churns like molten lava beneath the surface of our pain. *Why did this happen?* Most of us know this is not a question that can ever be answered, but we need to voice it anyway. And the last things we want or need to hear are platitudes, some of which have been mentioned earlier. Embedded in the question of why is both a cry for meaning and an acknowledgment of all we cannot know. When it comes to death, it is an inherently rhetorical question, a shout from the knees with an upturned face, whether we believe there is One who hears or not. *Why this? Why him? Why her? Why now?* This is how the heart bleeds in words. And the only thing that can begin to stem the bleeding is a listening ear, not more words.

Before Rabbi Harold Kushner asked the question of why bad

things happen to good people, there was Job. In the biblical story, he was a man who endured suffering of every kind. Devout, righteous, prosperous, healthy, a family man with many friends, Job proceeded to lose everything. If anyone deserved to ask why, it was Job. And he did. His friends tried to supply the answers, but they not only fell short, they made him feel worse. "You get what you deserve" was one of the things they inferred. Great. The other was "Stop complaining. This must be God's plan." Also not helpful.

Like Job, when bad things happen to us, we look to God, we look to our friends, we look at ourselves, and we ask why. When uttered by the bereaved, it's a cry of lament, a mother's primal keen, a fist shaken toward the heavens—why? Although finding an answer to this question wouldn't change anything, many of us feel the need to ask it. Trying to come up with a reasonable explanation for loss is a way to break the free fall of pain. It delays and distracts us, momentarily, from the deep heartbreak that is waiting in the silence.

Most of us can understand concrete cause and effects, the routine "if this, then thats" in our everyday lives. We tell children not to touch a hot stove. Why? Because they could get burned. It makes sense. We have reasons for doing the things we do, and if asked why, most of us could probably give a sensible answer. Even nature, in all its terrifying power, follows basic principles that give the world order and structure. If a natural disaster occurs—a tsunami or an earthquake, for example—scientists can study weather patterns, fault lines, and the shifting tides. They can help us understand why the earth moved, but they cannot tell us why our loved ones were caught in the storm. And this is the question we want answered most of all. We demand a reason for why things happen, as if finding a cause and effect would make the pain go away. At those times, we call God into our office (even if we haven't talked for a while), sit God down, and tap our pencils, waiting for an answer as to why our loved ones died. We forget that God doesn't need to run anything by us for our approval. God does not maliciously send us pain, nor does God exit out the back door at the first sign of trouble. Instead, God hunkers down in the dark with us and is ready to catch us when we fall. In the words of Rabbi Kushner,

> God does not cause our misfortunes. Some are caused by bad luck, some are caused by bad people, and some are simply an inevitable consequence of our being human and being mortal, living in a world of inflexible natural laws. The painful things that happen to us are not punishments for our misbehavior, nor are they in any way part of some grand design on God's part. Because the tragedy is not God's will, we need not feel hurt or betrayed by God when tragedy strikes. We can turn to Him for help in overcoming it, precisely because we can tell ourselves that God is as outraged by it as we are.*

I find comfort in the idea that God is as outraged as we are. Somehow it reminds me that we are in this together, God and I.

Why do terrible things happen? Why did our loved ones have to

---

* Harold S. Kushner, *When Bad Things Happen to Good People* (New York: Schocken Books, 1981), 180.

die? We may never know the answers to these questions until we join those we love on the other side. Maybe when we get there it won't matter so much. Getting stuck on the question of why is like driving a car into a ditch. The more we rev the engine and spin the tires, the deeper the car sinks in the mud and the less likely we are to get it out. At some point we must consider another approach if we hope to ease our way back onto the road. Instead of asking over and over again why something has happened, perhaps we could ask how we might respond to it with courage and hope. If we do this, *why* no longer becomes a question, as in, "Why did this happen?" Rather, it becomes an active noun, something that points to a higher purpose for living. In the words of Nietzsche (quoted by Viktor Frankl in *Man's Search for Meaning*), "He who has a *why* to live for can bear almost any *how*."* The challenge is finding our *why*.

Frankl, an Austrian neurologist and psychiatrist who survived three years in various Nazi concentration camps, was well acquainted with death and unanswerable questions. During his time as a prisoner, he suffered unthinkable loss, deprivation, and sorrow. One snowy morning as the sun was dawning, and at a moment of complete despair, the image of his wife came to him. He did not yet know that she had already died in another camp. Describing the experience, he later wrote,

> But my mind clung to my wife's image, imagining it with an
> uncanny acuteness. I heard her answering me, saw her smile,

---

* Viktor E. Frankl, *Man's Search for Meaning: An Introduction to Logotherapy,* 4th ed., trans. Ilse Lasch (Boston: Beacon Press, 1992), 109.

her frank and encouraging look. . . . I understood how a man
who has nothing left in this world still may know bliss, be it
only for a brief moment, in the contemplation of his beloved.*

Frankl's love for his wife gave him more than a moment of
bliss—it gave him a reason to live. Instead of remaining in the endless,
unanswerable spiral of asking why he had to suffer such unspeakable
cruelty, he was determined to find meaning, even in the midst of his
suffering. He found that in the love he had for his wife. Her image
became part of his *why,* helping him find the strength and the *how* to
survive.

When devastating loss threatens to do us in, having taken what
we most love in life, we often struggle to find a reason to live. Invariably, the most enduring reasons to keep on living are grounded in
love. We may feel that our loved ones would *want* us to live. We may
decide to persevere out of love for our children or grandchildren. We
may have a task that still needs to be completed or a creative endeavor
that calls to us, something that is essential to our souls. Whatever our
why, when we find it and allow it to come into sharp focus, we can
begin to figure out our *how.*

How are we to go on? Sometimes strength is found in continuing
activities that were important to a loved one, such as championing a
cause or coaching a child's team. Sometimes it is in the simple commitment to keep up the garden that the one who died had worked so
hard to cultivate and maintain. Some who have lost wives or mothers

---

* Frankl, *Man's Search for Meaning,* 48–49.

or daughters to breast cancer find meaning in raising awareness or in participating in activities like Race for the Cure.

Rebecca Kowalski, who lost her beautiful son, Chase, in the Sandy Hook Elementary School shooting in 2012, wondered how she could go on after this. She and her family found their *how* by creating the CMAK (Chase Michael Anthony Kowalski) Sandy Hook Memorial Foundation. It is inspired by Chase's life and honors his memory with its vision to "turn tragedy into triumph by healing and strengthening our families and communities."* In putting love out into the world, and by doing good for others, they are reclaiming some of the goodness that was taken from them. This keeps their inner flames burning and helps give them a reason to go on.

When we stop *asking* why and instead begin to *find* our *why,* we can start mapping out our *how.* And something will begin to heal inside of us. Some people are afraid of healing. They mistakenly think healing means letting their loved ones go and leaving them in the past. This is not true. As we heal, we are better able to carry our loved ones with us because our arms are open. We are open. And in that openness the energy and love that is our son or daughter, our husband or sister will begin to seep in the cracks of our parched and weary hearts.

As for Job, the stand-in for all of us who suffer, the lesson is really about remembering that we are never alone. We can question God, life, and one another about why things happen as they do. We can, with good reason, lament the painful things that happen to us. But we also have the opportunity to respond with courage and with faithful-

---

* "CMAK Foundation," www.cmakfoundation.org.

ness. It takes courage to accept the deaths of our loved ones. It takes courage to live with the trauma of loss. By living, however, we have the opportunity to affirm that life is meaningful, that *our* lives are meaningful, and that the end of one life—even one we hold dear—does not necessitate the permanent cessation of happiness. As Frankl wrote, "At any moment, man must decide, for better or for worse, what will be the monument of his existence."* Living with courage and hope is perhaps the best monument we could build in honor of the gift of life and those we have loved.

Meditation: Today I will quiet the parts of me that clamor for knowing why my loved one died. Instead, I will meditate on how to survive with courage and hope.

Affirmation: I can find a reason to live, even with this loss.

---

* Frankl, *Man's Search for Meaning*, 124.

Touch has a memory.

—John Keats

Xs and Os

Even the most spiritual people live in a body. That's an inextricable part of the human condition. Our souls inhabit bodies that are formed in our mother's wombs and that emerge completely helpless and vulnerable. Suddenly, there are a variety of senses for us to explore, ways in which to experience the world around us, aspects of this newfound physicality that come with being encased in bodies. We don't spend whatever time we have here on the planet trying to get out of them; in fact, most people try to stay in their bodies as long as they can. We aspire to integrate the parts of who we are and to understand what it is to be a created being as well as a spiritual being.

There must be something the soul needs to learn by incarnating, or else what's the point of this round-trip journey? Apparently it's harder than it looks to grow into what we were created to be. Animals seem to do this pretty flawlessly. A lion knows what it means to be a lion, an eagle expands its wings in eagle-like fashion, and a dog is doggedly loyal. Humans, on the other hand, seem to have a harder time acting humanely. When we were created, God called us "good." Left to our own devices, we often fall short. Perhaps that's why God felt compelled to come down to earth and show us how it's done. Before the world was formed, this part of God was called the Word. Incarnated, it was called Jesus. We all know how that turned out. Still, we try. We do our best with whatever time we have to become who God created us to be. In order to do this, we need each other.

God has given us bodies for a reason. God has given us life so that we might be a reflection of God's light and love on earth. It's no small miracle that these perishable bodies are able to contain a spirit for any length of time. But through them, we have the opportunity to experience unique aspects of God's love. We can feel God's compassion when we show compassion to others. We can sense God's delight when we delight in the beauty of what God has created. We can experience God's kindness and mercy when we extend kindness to a stranger. And we can know God's tenderness in the tender touch of another person.

The body is the vessel through which we come to know and love one another, and it is the body that we miss when the spirit departs. That's the trouble with wanting to hold on to the perishable parts of each other. It's quite a bind. Most of us trust that the soul is immortal, that our loved ones have not entered into a void, and we hope to one day be reunited with them. The trouble is, we miss them when they are not physically here with us. We might still feel their presence when they are gone, but we also long to feel the warmth of their bodies next to us. This is not a failure of the human spirit; it's how God made us.

Part of what it means to be human is to love one another with all the senses we have. Couples pledge "to have and to hold" each other for life. Most of us like physical contact. We like to hug and to kiss, to snuggle with our kids, and to take the hand of a friend. We are tactile creatures, and we need to be touched.

Touch is something that we share as human beings, whether we are sighted or blind, whether we are deaf or can hear. You always remember your first kiss, or the brush of your lips against a baby's head, or a loved one's embrace that you never wanted to end. You can probably still feel what it was like to cuddle on the couch or to walk down the street hand in hand, to rock your child to sleep or to be rocked yourself. We sign our letters with Xs and Os because love is a whole-bodied thing. We kiss and hug, and we draw our loved ones close in a beautiful mash of emotion and physicality—and it is one of the hardest things to do without after someone we love dies. When I asked a ninety-year-old woman what she would do if she could go back in time before her husband died, she told me, "I would spend more time lounging next to him in bed and not be in such a hurry to get up. And I would give him more foot rubs." The joy of sensory connection and the comfort of another's physical presence are like embers that continue to glow long after the bonfire of youth has calmed to a passionate simmer. The touch of a beloved's hand is singular. It is instantly recognizable and cannot be replaced.

This simple truth hit me squarely in the heart while I was sitting with a woman who had recently lost her husband. An Italian Catholic in her late sixties, she was gracious and soft spoken, beautiful and welcoming. From the moment she opened the door to her home, I felt the warmth of family seeping from every room, like the aroma of fresh-baked bread. Initially, I wasn't sure she would be open to the support of an outside person, much less one who was a stranger and a Protestant chaplain. She had a close-knit, supportive family that included three grown children living nearby. But she was always gracious, allowing me to visit as part of her husband's hospice team while he was alive and as a friend after he died.

As we sat together, surrounded by pictures emanating a lifetime of love, the absence of her husband was palpable. He had been a bull of a man, physically strong and wholly dedicated to his family, while she was pretty and petite, with perfect almond eyes and a wide smile. His Sicilian accent had been harder for me to decipher than the soft lilt of her southern Italian, and she often had to translate for me when he was most animated in his storytelling. I was conscious of the fact that they didn't really need me there but had welcomed me out of hospitality, and they were forgiving of any fumbles as I tried to offer comfort. Now that he was gone, the house was so still. If absence had a sound, it would have been booming.

Searching for ways to help her speak about her loss, I asked the woman what she missed most about her husband. "I miss his touch," she said quietly. Her eyes grew soft, and I could tell that behind them images of private moments were unspooling. We let the words hover in the air before dissipating into the afternoon sun. And I felt that I had been given a glimpse of hidden treasure. She was a private person, one who didn't share intimate thoughts freely, and I suspect her husband had been the same way. Their life was centered on the family, but their relationship was its own universe. In fact, her son later said he had never seen his parents exchange a sensuous touch—and yet this is what she missed. Perhaps the outward expression of this deep intimacy was the one thing they did not share with the family. It was theirs and theirs alone.

We cannot replace the touch of a loved one, whether it is our beloved's caress or the sweet hug of a child. "Touch has a memory," wrote Keats. In the absence of touch, however, our hearts still remember. The feel of a loved one's hand leaves an imprint when it is gone, a crevice that remains empty and cannot be filled by another's. Perhaps as we are dying, we will feel that same hand filling the empty grooves perfectly, like a puzzle piece that has been missing for years. We will recognize it instantly and take it joyfully, and we will trust where it is leading us.

Meditation: Today I will shut my eyes, remembering the touch of my loved one with gratitude.

Affirmation: I am a spirit living in a body; both need to be honored and nurtured.

Yesterday

When what feels like the best parts our lives are in the rearview mirror, the future can seem as if it's there too. Grief pulls us into the past, leaving us banging on its locked door, the door to the place where our loved ones seem to have gone. No matter how much we long to go back there, no matter how hard we knock, we can never reenter a world that has already been. This reality can be so difficult to accept after a loss. Each day may feel like an eternity, dragging us further and further away from the last moments we had with our loved ones. We want to go back in time. Of course we do! We know what has been. And we yearn to squeeze our way through the crack in time that still allows a glimmer of that light to slip through.

The moments that I feel this yearning for the past don't always have to do with the death of a loved one. Looking at photos of my children when they were small can prompt it. I miss the feel of their little bodies wrapped around mine like baby koala bears. The sleepy head on my shoulder, the small hand in my hand—all these live in my sensory memory. Still, there are times that I long for one more moment of being able to hold my children (who are now in their twenties) or rest with them in the crook of my arm. Those days are gone, but I am so grateful that I had them. They exist in a past that shimmers with happy memories, and they imbue the present with layers of color, texture, and light. In the case of a death, however, the past takes on even more significance. The inability to share more times together and to create more memories can make the present feel like an empty room and the future look like a spool of black thread, unraveling in endless dark circles.

Death does not give us the option to remain with our loved ones. It takes away this choice. But it cannot take away how we choose to live in the present or what hopes we might envision for the future. Despite our sorrow, we can aspire to greet the present moment with gratitude and to look to the horizon with optimism, or we can succumb to the yearning for all we cannot change. Yearning for yesterday will neither bring it back nor bring us joy. So how do we hold on to the happiness we've known without living in the past?

Perhaps the first thing we can do is to acknowledge that there is, in reality, no such thing as living in the past. If there were, many brokenhearted people would be hopping the first train there. We are always living in the present moment; that's all we have. But the present is not empty. Our internal sanctuaries cannot be robbed of what has already been or the treasure trove of memories we bring to everything we do and all that we see. Yesterday may be a time to which we can never go back, but it is also the guardian of what can never be taken from us—each moment shared and every tender word exchanged. We will always have these. When we are grieving, however, reaching for things in the past can be like stuffing our pockets with make-believe gold. We think the real gold lies behind us when, in reality, it lies within.

A woman whose husband had died was faced with the prospect of moving. On the one hand, the house was comfortably familiar and the last she would ever share with him, at least here on earth. On the other hand, it had become an obstacle course of pain. Every room seemed trip-wired to broadcast her husband's absence. The chair in the den was no longer *his* chair; it was his *empty* chair. The closet no longer held his clothes, and his dresser contained only a few scattered remnants. Even the road leading up to the house was emotionally treacherous for her, especially the stretch where she had always called to let him know she was almost home. Some days she felt isolated and trapped in the house by his absence, and other days she felt comforted by the reverberations of his presence and of their life together.

When she finally decided to move, for a variety of emotional and financial reasons, she was still torn. Would she be leaving him behind? Could she move somewhere without him for the first time in her adult life? She was lamenting the difficulties inherent in her decision when a friend tried to encourage her by suggesting this could be the start of a whole new life. "But I don't want a new life," she cried. "I want my old one." It is painfully normal to yearn for the life we knew before the deaths of our loved ones. Those who have not yet lost someone dear to them may not fully understand this. Facing the fact that we cannot have what and whom we want most is perhaps the hardest thing we will ever do—and it takes tremendous courage. Accepting that our lives are ongoing and still worth living is no small task.

Sometimes the past that we visit over and over again carries painful memories: the last breath of a loved one, an ambulance ride, the telephone ring that came in the night, harsh words exchanged without knowing they'd be the last. When yesterday comes suddenly, as the Beatles sang, it can haunt us. What do we do with the images that inflict fresh wounds every time they come into our minds? If we suppress them, they can spring up unexpectedly, like a beach ball that is submerged in the water and then released. Maybe it's better to leave them floating quietly on the surface for a time. Or maybe, when a painful memory comes to mind, we can do more than simply try to hold it at bay or stuff it back into the jack-in-the-box.

One technique I have recommended to people, especially those who cannot seem to get upsetting recurring images out of their heads, draws from a variety of contemplative practices. It can be used to quiet one's mind before prayer or to loosen the hold of a traumatic memory. Many grief-stricken people have told me they have found the suggestion helpful. When an upsetting image comes to mind, one should acknowledge—not suppress—it before trying to let it go. Imagine, for example, sitting on the banks of a peaceful river. If a leaf should fall into the water, you might notice it, but you do not have to follow it with your gaze as it floats downstream. So, too, with traumatic memories. When they surface, we can acknowledge them but we do not have to chase after them. We can honor them as part of the mosaic of who we are, and then choose a different colored tile, a beautiful memory, for example, to be our touchstone for the day. When the painful thought comes, we can say, *Yes, I see you. But today I choose to hold in my mind a different image.* This might be something like the color of the sky on a particular day, perhaps, or that of your loved one laughing. A happy image, consciously chosen, can help release us from the fetters of pain, at least temporarily. It functions like a prayer that is taped to the sun visor of a car. When our eyes become blinded by tears, we can pull it down to cut the glare and to help us move forward.

If your heart still pounds because you cannot get an upsetting picture out of your mind, you can re-center by taking a few deep breaths and by handing it over to God. Ask God to hold it in safekeeping. See how clearly you can picture yourself releasing the disturbing image into God's gentle hands. What are you wearing? What kind of day is it? What does God look like? Sit for a bit. Have a chat. Can you hear what God is saying to you? If it's still too noisy to hear God's voice with the ears of your heart, you can try quieting your mind by counting your breaths. This practice is used by people of many faiths. Sitting comfortably with eyes shut and jaw relaxed, begin by breathing through your nose. Focus your attention on the point of entry for the breath and count each inhalation and exhalation. Begin with one and count up to ten. If you get distracted, don't worry; just start over. Do this in a cycle of ten, over and over, until you feel your mind start to clear and your body relax. Even a few minutes of practice a day can help to quiet your mind and to make room for God's comfort to surround you.

Practices like this and others, such as Centering Prayer, developed by Christian monastic Thomas Keating, can help us cope with the past, stay in the present, and open ourselves to inspiration and guidance. Influenced by his exposure to Eastern meditation practices and grounded in the ancient Christian teachings of the Desert Fathers, Keating created the following four guidelines to Centering Prayer:

1. Choose a sacred word as a symbol of your intention to consent to God's presence and action within.

2. Sitting comfortably, (but not too comfortably which may induce sleep) your back straight and with your eyes closed, settle briefly and then silently introduce the sacred word as a symbol of your intention to consent to God's presence and action within.

3. When you engage with thoughts, return ever so gently to the sacred word.

4. At the end of the prayer period, remain in silence for a few minutes with your eyes closed.*

What happens in prayer and meditation is an opening of the heart and the soul. This is so important when one is struggling with loss. Death can prompt a slamming of the interior door. We don't want to open it because doing so means living without the ones we love. Prayer helps loosen the lock. It allows oxygen to flow back into our spirits after being depleted by grief. We take that first deep breath when we accept what has happened. In doing so, we are no longer suffocated by our yearning for the past. Grateful for all that has been, for the beauty and love we have known, we can begin to live again.

---

* Contemplative Outreach Ireland, "The Method of Centering Prayer," www
.contemplativeoutreachireland.com/centering-prayer/the-method-of-centering-prayer/.

Meditation: Today I will gently tuck my memories into the sacred place reserved for them. I will sit quietly with God and trust that I am being cared for.

Affirmation: The past is light enough for me to carry without effort when I open my heart to the present.

We are such stuff
As dreams are made on, and our little life
Is rounded with a sleep.

—William Shakespeare, *The Tempest*

Zzzz

Sleep and death have been entwined for centuries in human consciousness, the relationship between them often explored in mythology and literature. When we are extremely tired, we fall into a "dead sleep." When we die, we "rest in peace." Such is the tumbling back and forth between these states in our efforts to understand and accept them. For the bereaved, sleep can be elusive; for the dying, it can be frightening. The first can have trouble getting or staying asleep; the second can be afraid of never waking up. At an open-coffin wake, there is an effort to make the deceased appear as if he or she is merely sleeping. When we need to compassionately assist our pets in their dying process, we say we are "putting them to sleep." In Greek mythology, sleep and death are twins—and both are a little menacing. Sleep, like death, is ultimately unavoidable, no matter how long we try to hold it off. Part of being human, then, is accepting that we are made to rest and we are made to die—and yet saying "good night" is clearly different from saying "good-bye." Sleep is temporary; death is not.

While making funeral arrangements for my father, I asked to see his body before it was prepared for the service. Because I wasn't there when he died, I felt compelled to see him as soon as I could. The funeral director was hesitant, gently explaining to me that Dad wasn't "ready," meaning embalmed. That was fine with me. I explained to him that I had seen many, many dead bodies as a hospice chaplain and that I wanted to see my father's. After a few minutes, I was led into a closet-sized room. Dad's body was there, covered up to his bare shoulders in a white sheet. I wouldn't say he looked like he was sleeping, but he looked beautiful to me. His face was in repose, his expression relaxed and untroubled. I took in the large incision on his neck that appeared newly stitched together. It was where he had been cut in preparation for the dialysis that never transpired. It pained me to see it, as I imagined him having to suffer that. I found myself wondering what went through his mind during those last hours, those last minutes. And what kept coming to me were the words *he knew, he knew*. Standing beside his now-still frame, I could feel the warmth and the wisdom of his spirit. I felt him next to me, as if we were both taking in the dear frame he had inhabited. I didn't want him to be asleep because sleep would mean he was still in that body, still a prisoner of what could no longer contain his enormous spirit. No, he was not asleep. He was awake and he was standing beside me.

I touched his hair. I took his hand. I had always loved his hands. They were healing hands. His palms were wide, his fingers strong and straight. Whenever he placed them on my head to comfort me when I was a little girl, or to pray for me, as he did after I'd lost my hair to chemotherapy, they emitted an unmistakable energy. Now they were quiet and cool. When I was born, the doctor placed me in these hands even before my mother's. In so many ways, they were home to me. He looked beautiful the way an abalone shell looks beautiful: the iridescence was stunning but the shell was empty. The dear and familiar casing was all that remained of the person I knew as my dad. And the lingering shimmer was surely from the holiness that had resided there. I knew once he was embalmed, it would be gone, and so I took my time honoring the home he had inhabited for seventy-nine years. Without it, I would not have been able to hug him or to hear his voice, to be carried when I was a child or to hold his arm when he walked me down the aisle. But it was immanently clear that he was no longer there, in that body, and that he was not asleep.

I do not want the dead to sleep or to rest in peace. I want them to be awake and smiling, learning and growing. *"Wachet auf"* sings the chorus in Bach's cantata: "Wake up!"* If the spirit needs to rest, I can't imagine it would choose to do this in a body that is no longer working or in the particles of ash that once were connected by bone and sinew. And how could the spirit rest in the cool, dark confines of an earthen grave? The spirit is beyond both sleep and death. It is the eternal part of this mystery we know as human life. As Rumi

---

* BWV 140.

put it, "My soul is from elsewhere, I'm sure of that / and I intend to end up there."*

Just before Jesus famously called his friend Lazarus from the grave, he wept. Why? If he knew he could and would raise him from the dead, then what possible reason could he have for being sad? He understood what he was getting into before he arrived in Bethany. In fact, he had delayed traveling there, even though he knew Lazarus was ill. The disciples were not thrilled about going back to Bethany, where people had wanted to kill Jesus, but he was undeterred. "Lazarus is sleeping," Jesus told his faithful friends. "Well then, we don't need to rush," they reasoned. You can feel a deep, perhaps exasperated sigh when Jesus was forced to put it more bluntly, saying, "Lazarus is dead." When he arrived in Bethany, Martha, the sister of Lazarus, ran to greet him, giving him the sad news. He reassured her, offering a powerful proclamation of his identity. But when little sister Mary ran out and fell on her knees in tears, Jesus lost it. The original language describes him as literally shuddering with emotion, prompting those around Jesus to remark, "See how he loved him!"†

It's precisely because Jesus loved Lazarus that he wept. I'm just not sure he was upset about him dying. He knew he could fix that right up. I believe Jesus wept because he knew what he was about to ask of Lazarus, namely, to leave the eternal realm, the home of our spirits, the place to which our souls have been traveling since we breathed our first breath, and to return to human life. What a tall

---

* Coleman Barks, trans., *The Essential Rumi* (New York: HarperCollins, 1995), 2.
† See John 11:1–36.

order for Laz. After all, he'd made it. He'd made the transition out of the body, and he was free from the confines of this world. Then, from a distance we will never be able to fathom, Lazarus heard the familiar voice of his dear friend calling, "Come out!" This is a story of Jesus's authority over life and death, but it is also a testimony to the power of friendship. I'd like to think Lazarus had a say in the matter. Maybe he took a last lingering look over his shoulder toward heaven and let out a wistful sigh before surrendering to the voice that was calling him. Maybe he could have said, "Not now! Remember, I'm sleeping! [Wink, wink]." But he didn't. Whether out of love or friendship, loyalty or obedience, Lazarus said, "Okay." He eased back into that old body, the one that had been rotting for four days, and he stepped out of the cave like a mummy, one who didn't even have to yell, "Boo!"

When I sleep, I don't want to die, and when I die, I don't want to sleep. But the thing is, it's not in our hands. In order to cope with the uncertainties inherent in the mystery, it helps to see both sleep and death as gifts that are offered to the soul when there are no alternatives. We need to rest. Grief is exhausting. Pain is exhausting. Even when one is grieving, perhaps *especially* when one is grieving, sleep is important. Surrender to it. Be grateful for it. Get help when you need it. Find your loved one in a dream. And as you think about the ones who have died, do not picture them asleep under the ground or scattered to the wind; think of them as vibrant and glowing, living now among the saints of light, part of God's cosmic consciousness. They are well and they are happy—and they wait with open arms to greet you. Find a prayer to connect you, like a rope running between two tin cans. Speak into your end and listen for the voice at the other.

When I was a little girl, the prayer I whispered into my end of the rope was,

> Now I lay me down to sleep,
> I pray the Lord my soul to keep.
> If I should die before I wake,
> I pray the Lord my soul to take.

It is pretty alarming, really, when you think about it. Every night, as I prepared for sleep, I was also preparing for the possibility of not waking up. What's more, the idea of the Lord taking my soul was also a bit unnerving. I mentioned this to my mom one night—the dying and the soul taking. I didn't want to be taken anywhere. I wanted to wake up in my bed in the morning, just like every other morning. She assured me that the prayer was purely precautionary. She didn't say those exact words, but that was the gist of it. While still slightly unsettled, I took her at her word and continued to pray it each night.

Now, all these many years later, I trust that my soul *is* in God's keeping. And if I do not wake in my bed, I hope the Lord takes my spirit-hand and leads me to where God is, to where my loved ones are, and to that place from which my soul came. Death is not the big sleep. It is but a swinging door through which our spirits pass. We will all have a turn to come bursting into the heavenly party. Until that time, let's remember to rest.

Meditation: Tonight before I go to sleep, I will picture my loved ones walking with God and enjoying the company of others who have gone before them.

Affirmation: Waking or sleeping, I am in God's care.

Acknowledgments

Thanks, always, to Cynthia Manson, the best agent and friend a writer could have. Your faith in me makes me work harder and aspire to be a better writer. You believed in me when I hardly believed in myself. I am so grateful for you.

Deep gratitude is extended to John Blase and the team at Water-Brook. John, your wise and gentle guidance has shaped this book in ways both great and small. Thank you for your expert eye, your encouragement, and for giving this book wings. Immeasurable thanks to Kathy Mosier. Your thoughtful attention to detail is reflected on every page. Although an editor's hand may be invisible to others, it is invaluable and so appreciated. Thank you to Mark Ford for the beautiful cover design and to Karen Sherry for the lovely interior design.

I would be remiss if I did not humbly acknowledge the profound influence that Frederick Buechner's work has had on me. His reflections on simple words, organized according to the alphabet, have long been my go-to when I have needed a boost of inspiration. I'm also indebted to him for giving me my best friend, Katherine.

I am profoundly grateful for every person who has sat around the bereavement table and those who have been willing to share their broken hearts with me. Thank you for entrusting me with your stories. Special thanks to my friend Chris Ulrich, who first taught me how to run a bereavement group. Your beautiful imprint is on everything I do well as a facilitator. Thank you for your love and friendship!

No words could express the gratitude I have for my parents, Dick and Lillian Ruehrwein, for the love they shared and for the love that endures even in death. Thank you, Mom, for living, even when you thought you could not, and for continuing to teach me about courage and faith. I am also grateful for my sisters, Laurie and Jennie, my brother Joey, and for brothers Ray and Jim, gone too soon but remembered always with love. We were the luckiest kids ever, weren't we? What we inherited will never be measured in dollars and cents. Dad left a treasure trove of love and faith.

Finally, to Andrew, Cat, and Alex—you are my lexicon of love.